DANIEL STEWART

From the portrait by Raeburn in the Merchants' Hall.

A HISTORY

OF

DANIEL STEWART'S COLLEGE

1855—1955

by

J. THOMPSON
History Master

DANIEL STEWART'S COLLEGE
EDINBURGH
1955

PRINTED IN GREAT BRITAIN BY
WADDIE AND CO. LTD.
EDINBURGH AND LONDON

CONTENTS

LIST OF ILLUSTRATIONS

PREFACE

THE writing of this account of the growth of Daniel Stewart's College during the first century of its life was suggested to me by Dr. Robbie. The work has been made agreeable by the help I have received from all sides. Dr. Robbie has found evidence and cited witnesses, suggested lines of approach, read the manuscript, and seen to all the business side of the publication. The Merchant Company Education Board has given me access to the relevant official records, but the members are in no way responsible for any expressions of opinion in this history; their secretary, Mr. Harvey M. Jamieson, and the Old Master, Mr. A. Dick Wood, read the manuscript and suggested many improvements. The same service has been done by Mr. Frank Ross, by the vice-convener, Mr. A. V. Scott, and by Mr. C. W. Gardner, a former secretary of the Stewart's College Club, who has also read the proofs.

Three parts of the book are by other hands. The first two chapters are substantially the work of Mr. W. F. Ritchie, principal classics master in Arbroath High School, who did a great deal of work on the early history of the school when he was a master here, and whose notes and articles in the Magazine were of very great help to me. The chapter on cricket was written by an F.P. who wishes to remain anonymous. (He will not escape recognition: one man only could have written it.) The chapter on football is basically the work of Mr. A. Balfour Kinnear. Mr. T. D. Adie brought it up to date and added some new material, as well as supplying the information about the Golf Club.

To innumerable F.P.s and members of the staff I am indebted for information, either in the form of written memoranda—how astonishingly good some memories are—or given in reply to questions. I cannot hope to set down here the names of all who have helped me in this way. To some I have acknowledged my debt in the text. Will the others accept this expression of my gratitude?

Miss Robertson, our indispensable secretary, has had the trouble of typing the manuscript, and did me the further service of unearthing the Register of Foundationers.

THE ARCHITECT'S VISION

PERSPECTIVE VIEW OF THE STEWART'S HOSPITAL, EDINBURGH.
David Rhind Architect

[From a print in the Merchant's Hall.

DANIEL STEWART

THE only contemporary references to Daniel Stewart in print are found in the Edinburgh Directories and in an obituary notice in the *Scots Magazine* of 1814. The former merely state that he is a Macer in the Court of Exchequer, and frequently give his name and address in the normal lists. The latter is more instructive and reads as follows: " 31st May. At Windmill Street, Daniel Stewart for many years one of the Macers at the Court of Exchequer, aged 73. The gentleman has left the great bulk of his fortune, acquired by industry and attention, for the establishment and support of Charitable Institutions." It is little enough, and suggests that he had chosen to live in comfortable obscurity. But a certain amount about him can be pieced together from other sources.

He was a Perthshire lad from Strathtay, probably Gaelic speaking. His father was a crofter at Wester Tober-an-donich in the parish of Dull, and his mother a MacFarlane from Logierait. But his date of birth in 1741 is not recorded in the parish register either of Logierait or Moulin, nor is it engraved on his tombstone. The family Bible in which it was doubtless written has long since disappeared. He had a brother John, whose daughter, Isabella, will be mentioned later. It was probably a descendant of this brother, John Stewart-Morton of Cheapside, who in 1889 wrote to the Merchant Company to ask permission to have the Raeburn portrait copied. He claimed to be the great grand-nephew and sole surviving male relation of Daniel Stewart. The permission was granted but whether the copy was made is uncertain.

No trace of the croft now remains, but towards the end of last century a small thatched barn used to be pointed out as the cottage in which the crofter Stewart and his family had lived. At an early age he began to work on the farm as a herd boy. Life was difficult, for the soil was thin and light. Nothing is known of his education but it has been said that "he wrote a good hand." Whatever his capabilities, he left his native parish and came to Edinburgh as a wig-maker's apprentice. The suggestion is made that one of the Maules of Panmure found him the position, but the connection may be legendary. The name of Maule, however, will recur often in this story, and it cannot always be accidental.

While working at the wig-maker's he attracted the attention of a client who was about to go to India. Daniel Stewart accepted the post of valet to this person and accompanied him on his voyage. The master died, leaving his faithful servant £11,000. (From this time we are a little more certain of dates.) In 1771 Daniel Stewart, now thirty years old, returned to Edinburgh and was appointed one of the Macers in the Court of Exchequer where Baron Maule of Inverkeillory was one of the judges. From 1776 he lived in Baron Maule's Close,* off the High Street, near the Nether Bow Port; from 1784(?)–93 he lived below Crichton's Entry in the Canongate, and from 1793–1814 at his own flat at 10 Windmill Street "in that district called 'Society,'" on the outer fringes of George Square. This flat remained in the hands of his Trustees and of the Merchant Company till 1887.† The office he held in the Exchequer Court was not an exalted one, though the salary was not inconsiderable.

The Court of Exchequer—it survived till 1856—presided over by the Lord High Treasurer of Great Britain, a Lord Chief Baron and four other Barons, looked after Customs and Excise Duties, inspected the accounts of Sheriffs, and collected Revenue. To attend Barons at all meetings of the Court three Macers were appointed who held their commissions during good behaviour. Their duties were to carry the Mace in and out of Court, to make proclamations in Court, attend Juries, take charge of witnesses and swear such persons as made affidavits before the Court. At first the salary was £80 per annum, but when Daniel Stewart was appointed the amount paid was only £50. Provision was made, however, so that the additional £30 could be collected in fees, carefully regulated by a table of charges. In 1880 he was appointed Deputy Court Mareschal, and in 1803 his salary was raised to £80 per annum.

The rest of our knowledge of the man is had from scattered, business sources, from his most illuminating Will and from his Trust Disposition and Deed of Settlement. About everything he took infinite pains and it comes as almost a relief to find him making a slip in his business dealings. A Minute of the Town Council (21/12/1812) shows that he had bought in 1782 a bake-house without realising that a feu duty of 10s. was payable on the vault. When the duty was demanded in 1805 he had this vault built up rather than pay, but later agreed to pay the arrears and to buy the feu. He appears, too, to have acted as a spare time factor

* Later called Society Close.

† The information about the house which Daniel Stewart occupied has been confirmed by a most patient and painstaking piece of research undertaken by Mr. Donald Macdonald, the City Assessor, who also prepared three very illuminating plans showing Windmill Street, the High Street, and the Canongate in Daniel Stewart's time and now. This evidence and these plans have been deposited with the Headmaster.

for other people's property. The other minor references can speak for themselves.

From the Minute Book of the Calton Trades (entry of 27th October 1803) we read "The Box-master reported that he had sold to Mr. Daniel Stewart of His Majesty's Court of Exchequer 12 yards 1 foot and 6 inches of the Burying Ground, bounded on the South by the South Dyke, on the west and east by unpurchased Ground, on the North by the property of Dick. That the Price, at the rate of £2, 2/- Sterg. per yard, amounts in all to £25, 10s. sterg. which was paid to the Boxmaster." This transaction was approved, and the ground—it lies at the end of the central path—was allotted as a burial place to Mr. Daniel Stewart and his heirs and representatives in all time coming.

Having decided "to devote his Funds to the Foundation of a Hospital for Boys" he began to make preparations for this by having his portrait painted by the foremost Scottish painter of the day, Mr. (later Sir) Henry Raeburn. Raeburn's studio was the home of wit and intellectual conversation, and everybody entered his studio in the happiest frame of mind and went away pleased that they looked so well on canvas. It was the artist's common practice to carry on a conversation with the sitter, and quite often there were visitors who joined in those discussions. It would be an interesting but rather difficult task to compose an imaginary conversation to suit the occasion.

Two letters from Henry Raeburn about the portrait are still extant. Because they give us some insight into Daniel Stewart's character they are quoted in their entirety. In the first letter we learn that Stewart disliked debts; in the second we find the painter trying to pacify an angry client, who was demanding to know why his portrait had not been exhibited along with Raeburn's others. Here is a rather curious twist of character from what we have usually supposed. The quiet, unobtrusive Daniel wishes to be exhibited in the company of the fashionable beauties and men of high social and intellectual standing.

YORK PLACE, 18*th November*, 1812·

"DEAR SIR,

I have the pleasure of your letter, and my cold (I thank you) is better, and I will with much pleasure wait on you on Friday. My price for a picture of the size of yours is 100 gns. It would be a great deal in my pocket if everybody was as anxious to be out of debt as you are. I am with great esteem,

Dear Sir,

Your most obedient servant,

HENRY RAEBURN.

DEAR SIR,

  I am sorry you have been so ill and so long confined. I have been much engaged or I would have been out to enquire for you. Your picture is not in the Exhibition—as I never take it upon me to put a picture there without the person expresses some wish for it,—many people have an aversion at it, which begging their pardon appears to me very foolish. When the Exhibition first began here, I put in some pictures without thinking and gave offence, and since then I have made it a rule to run no risk of that kind again. But besides this I can only get in a very limited number—some that I had in measure promised for I have not been able to get in. Your picture I bestowed particular pains upon and I should have been very well pleased it had been exhibited, but what I have said above is the real state of the case.

      I remain, Yours sincerely,

       HENRY RAEBURN."

  There were two others in his household at Windmill Street— his housekeeper, Janet Livingstone, and his servant, Janet Gaire. For Janet Livingstone he provided well in his Will. She married one of the men to whom Daniel Stewart had lent money, a Mr. Jobson of Sheffield, and appears to have had a family, for in 1888 G. Jobson Marples of Ecclesall, near Sheffield, asked the Merchant Company if he might have a clock, once the property of Daniel Stewart, and got it. Janet Gaire fared less well, and his words about her raise all sorts of speculations about the household in Windmill Street and throw an unkindly light on the man. He left a holograph memoir dated 12th March 1813, which runs:

  "Janet Gaire my Servant has been in my service for Twenty eight years past: She is a malicious ill hearted person as ever was in any honest man's house; She behaved very rudely to my poor misfortunate niece, and when I was in distress seven years ago, she used every person ill that came about me. She abused Miss Livingstone and made her life bitter, and almost drove her from the House: She treats Miss Livingstone always very ill when I am in great distress: She has made in my Service One Hundred & Fifteen pounds Sterling . . . From all the foregoing circumstances I shall not leave her any annuity. Let her take her own money and live upon it at the rate of Five Shillings a week, and that will serve her well; and if she lives to spend her own money at that rate, I then authorise and empower my Trustees to pay to her per week Five Shillings sterling out of my funds and Bury her decently. I desire this to be read to her after my death."

  It is a waspish letter with a nasty sting.

  During the last years of his life his niece, Isabella Stewart, "who laboured under great debility and derangement of mind" was his special care. Her father had died about 1800, and though she was boarded with a Mrs. Wright "in a comfortable house at the Dean," Daniel Stewart looked after her affairs and saw to her material needs. He had a good eye for a painting, and gathered together a small but admirably selected collection which he intended should be hung in his hospital.

Such are the known facts about Daniel Stewart. During his bachelor life he sometimes emerged from his seclusion to transact business, and these occasions are happily recorded. The Raeburn portrait and the obituary notice are the only contemporary opinions of him. "The portrait" it has been said, "shows him as he was in his seventy first year—a little ruddy-cheeked, white-haired man, dressed in decent, sober black, with knee-breeches and silver-buckled shoes: a quiet, demure, shrewd, kindly old gentleman." It conceals the man of the Janet Gaire letter.

But it is from his Trust Disposition and Deed of Settlement that we learn something of his character, his shrewdness and fore-sight, and, above all, his lofty ideal. He was an idealist, but at the same time realist enough to make sure that he had made adequate financial provision for the embodying of his high ideal in permanent, material form. He had taken such good care of his inheritance, or put it to such good use, as to have almost doubled it at the time of his death. He was meticulous in all he did, pondering over matters, now apparently trifling, and planning everything with wise insight. He had one besetting desire—to found an Institution for the sons of needy parents. It was not an original desire— Mary Erskine, George Heriot, George Watson to mention only the names known in Edinburgh, had thought of it before him. Edinburgh has been particularly blessed with public spirited bene-factors who endowed Education with their substance and gave many poor children benefits they would otherwise have missed. During his lifetime Daniel Stewart was quiet, unassuming and unknown. At his death, however, he added his name to the list of Edinburgh benefactors.

DANIEL STEWART'S WILL

DANIEL STEWART died on the 31st May 1814, and he was buried on the 3rd June. His funeral was attended by "all the respectable gentlemen contained in a list made up and subscribed by the defunct on 18th March 1813 with one or two exceptions occasioned by indisposition," and it was "conducted in all other respects agreeably to the written instructions which the deceased had given several months before his death."

The first meeting of his Trustees took place on 4th June 1814 at 10 Windmill Street. There were present Archibald Campbell, younger of Ardyne; Adam Longmore, senior, of the Exchequer; Robert Stuart, Deputy Receiver General; Adam Longmore, junior, of the Exchequer; Robert Stuart, Deputy Presenter of Signatures in the Exchequer; and John Buchan, W.S., and Charles Moodie, of the Auditor's Office of the Exchequer. These last two were not Hospital Trustees. It will be noted that the majority had some connection with the Exchequer Court, but Archibald Campbell, younger, of Ardyne, referred to also as "my old friend," did not accept office. The fact that Daniel Stewart had a considerable amount of money to leave was no doubt known to them, but the exact nature of the Settlement may have surprised them. The Trust Disposition and Settlement is dated 3rd May 1811, and the codicil 13th February 1813. The purposes of the Disposition are three in number:—(1) the payment of debts and funeral expenses. (But note the added observation: "There will be little or no debts after my death, because I pay ready money for everything I buy.") (2) the payment of gifts and legacies: (3) the payments for the upkeep of his property.

There were likewise three main aims in the Settlement. The first made ample provision for his niece—the liferent and occupation of his house and an Annuity of £300. As a mark of affection and regard for his niece, he permitted and allowed her remains and those of her children and of their offspring to be interred in his Tomb or Burial Ground but he excluded all others from that privilege. The second recommended the building and endowing of a Free School in his native parish of Logierait. Then, thirdly, after all expenses were paid, all legacies donated, and the last two clauses fulfilled, the Trustees were to administer his estate until, by the sale of his bonds and of certain property they had at their disposal £40,000, in addition to £2,000 per year from investments. Not until this was assured were they to proceed with the principal aim —the erection of Daniel Stewart's Hospital for Boys.

At his death the Daniel Stewart Trust Estate was valued at £17,863, 12s. 8d., exclusive of certain shop and house properties, the gross Rental of which was £920 per annum. The Estate consisted of "Lands, Tenements, Shops, Cellars, Bonds, Government Stocks, and monies invested in public and private Banking and mercantile companies." There are no advisers or friends mentioned, and we are left to surmise that he himself was solely responsible for the buying of Bonds, the purchasing of property and for the lending of money to private individuals. The Trustees were instructed to sell what was moveable estate, lease what was heritable, but not to sell certain properties until at least one year after the Foundation of the Institution. These were "all situated in a very central part of the city of Edinburgh and if kept in proper repair, will always let at good rents, and contribute much to a permanent yearly income for supporting the Charitable Institution hereinafter mentioned."

Some of the instructions and "observations" contained in the Will may be of interest and give some indication of Daniel Stewart's character and foresight.

He instructed that Miss Janet Livingstone, his housekeeper, fourth daughter of Alexander Livingstone of Crosscauseway, to whom he left £300 sterling, should be allowed along with her servant to remain in the house at Windmill Street and should have the privilege of the cellars and "the use of what was in them." Of repairs to the property he observes: "as I pay ready money for everything I buy and I pay the tradespeople I employ for repairing my properties when the work is done, I recommend it to my Trustees to do the same and the work will be well done and cheaper, and if it is a large piece of work to get estimates from different tradesmen and whoever does the work well and cheapest to prefer him."

He laid down rules about the leasing of property, what share the tenants should be asked to bear of the cost of upkeep and what materials should be used for painting. "The rooms to be painted in oil when it is necessary as the tenant can wash the walls when dirty with cold water and after the water with gall and that will make them very clean and therefore will need painting but very seldom, say once in twelve years. There is no occasion for stamped leases, missive letters will answer the purpose for if the tenants prosper they will not change their situation, and if they fail, the lease goes for nothing."

He provided for the upkeep of his tomb requiring his Trustees "to paint in oil the door of my tomb every sixth year to preserve the wood and to engage a mason to examine the roof of the tomb every third year and if necessary to point it with 'Tarras' or plaister lime to keep the vault dry within."

The Hospital was founded "for the relief, maintenance and education of Poor Boys of the name of Stewart, of the name of MacFarlane, and of any other name, residing within the city of Edinburgh or suburbs thereof, including the town of Leith, the children of deserving parents whose circumstances in life do not enable them suitably to support and educate their children at other Schools." The only other qualification—a certificate from a Minister or Elder of the Church was required to back the claim —was to be born of "honest, industrious and well-behaved parents." Physicians and surgeons were also to report on the physical condition of the potential Foundationers. The entrance age was to be not less than seven years old and not more than ten, and accordingly the period of residence would range from seven to five years.

The Founder had clear ideas of what he wished taught. His curriculum consisted of "English, the principles of the Holy Christian Religion accompanied with prayer morning and evening, Writing, Arithmetic and Book-keeping, Latin and Mathematics." Great stress was also laid on the attendance at Public Worship of the Headmaster and the Foundationers. If the Trustees should at any time desire to alter the Rules and Regulations (those of George Watson's Hospital were to be taken as the model) the advice of the Professor of Divinity at Edinburgh University had to be asked in the event of equality of voting. Though the Headmaster had to be "a man of true Protestant Religion, well-affected to the Protestant Succession, fearing God and of honest life and conversation," no special instructions were laid down for the choice of the Assistants. Some difficulty arose over the creed of the Headmaster later. The schism which created the Free Church divided the Trustees and the casting vote of the Professor of Divinity was needed in 1853 to lay down that the Headmaster must belong to the Established Church. The ruling was set aside in 1864.

In the matter of site and style of building, the Founder merely insisted that they choose "a piece of suitable ground in a healthy situation and having a proper supply of soft water" and "erect thereon an Hospital built in the best manner and most approved plan; neat, handsome and commodious."

Once opened, the Hospital was to continue for five years under the guidance of the Trustees nominated in the Will, or later co-opted,

11 O'CLOCK BREAK.

and then "the perpetual management or government of the said Hospital, and Funds thereto belonging shall *ipso facto* devolve upon and be thereafter administered by the Master, Treasurer and Twelve Assistants of the Merchant Company of Edinburgh." To the Company Daniel Stewart left £300 "as an encouragement."

For the Hospital he reserved several of his most cherished treasures—his mahogany table, his large Folio Bible in two volumes, and his bloodstone seal with his coat of arms and motto. He made to the Hospital one further bequest of the greatest importance—his collection of portraits.

The various Trustees each received a gift—his large mahogany chair covered with leather and large brass nails, his large horn for holding snuff, his walking cane mounted with a silver head, with his initials upon it, etc. He desired his Trustees to keep his gold watch, chain and seals, four in number, for his niece, Isabella Stewart "if it please God to grant her again the blessing of a sound mind and the right use of her reason if she is not married and leave no children—for her lifetime only I give her my watch. If she does not recover within ten years after my death, at that period I do hereby legate, give and bequeath to Mr. Robert Stuart, Deputy Presenter of Signatures in Exchequer the said watch, chain and seals as a small reward for the great attention he paid me in my distress and towards the latter part of my life."

A special memorandum provided that the Trustees should dine "altogether once a year in a tavern at the expense of the Trust . . . Let this dinner continue yearly until all the Trustees I named are dead and after that let the dinner drop away as the Hospital falls under the management of the new Governors."

His Trustees continued Daniel Stewart's prudent investments. The funds were placed widely on good security, usually of land, for short periods at the high rate of interest prevailing in the troubled years after the end of the Napoleonic wars; and there were few losses. The Mr. Jobson whom Miss Livingstone had married died still owing £500 which could not be recovered and on the bankruptcy of the Marquis of Huntly in 1838 the Trustees recovered only £1,100 of the £5,000 they had lent. But these were exceptions.

One of their bonds is of special interest. Colonel Stewart of Garth in 1824 borrowed £14,000 in two bonds, one of £12,000 the other of £2,000. The bond for £2,000 was handed over to the Trustees of the Free School at Logierait as its endowment under the Will. By 1836 the Perthshire Trustees discharged the Edinburgh Trustees of all responsibility for the school. The building is still there, a private house now, stone built, with Stewart's arms and the date 1819 over the door. Like so many other Scottish village schools last century it went far beyond the three Rs, offering the two hundred and eighteen pupils of 1857 instruction in land-measuring, agricultural chemistry, Gaelic and practical gunnery. Some Greek, too, may have been taught: William McPherson, once the schoolmaster, lies in the churchyard with a Greek inscription on the stone erected by his former pupils to his memory. People still point out a ruckle of stones as the site of Wester Tober-an-Donich.

THE HOSPITAL I

HE death, on 11th December 1845 of Isabella Stewart, the niece so carefully provided for—she had been living in Dean village in reasonable comfort with a daily glass of wine—permitted the trustees at last to begin building. Their funds, helped in their rise by the high rates of interest in the unsettled years after 1815, had risen to about £80,000, and produced in 1845 some £2,800, in spite of the fall in the interest rate to 3½ per cent. The money was adequate, ground had been bought, but the trustees were reluctant to begin. One of them, Burn Murdoch, was very eager to apply the funds, with parliamentary sanction of course, to another purpose. He argued that it would be impossible to find enough deserving boys to fill a new hospital, that Edinburgh had already sufficient provision for such boys and that "Institutions of this nature, instead of being an advantage to the community were found to be quite the contrary." He proposed that the funds should be used to found a home for incurables, and to this the other trustees agreed. (It is worth noticing that the former home for incurables was called after another of the Trustees—the Longmore Hospital.) But obviously the Master, Treasurer and Assistants of the Merchant Company had to be consulted as ultimate governors. They agreed wholeheartedly with the Trustees' plans and appointed a small committee to work with them. But the hopes of both were dashed by the Lord Advocate whose advice was sought; he made it very plain that Parliament was most unlikely to agree to any alteration in the use of the trust funds. Rather reluctantly, then, the Trustees went on to build their Hospital.

In January 1848 David Rhind, whose Commercial Bank building in George Street was newly erected and much praised, was appointed architect and prepared plans in various styles, Gothic, Italian and Elizabethan. The Trustees approved the Elizabethan style—it was the cheapest too—and so secured for their Hospital, on a reduced scale, the plans which had received second prize when submitted for the new Houses of Parliament. By October estimates had been received and tenders placed, the main one with John Hutchison for the mason and woodwork. His name is worth recalling. He lost money on the contract and brought an action against the trustees later, but the walls still show that he was a great mason. And he lost no time. On the 13th of November 1848 he broke ground; on 16th January 1849 the first stone was laid and for the next three years carts were to rumble from the Craigleith quarries with stone to complete the work.

"Grand édifice élégamment construit
Que couronne un fouillis de tours et de tourelles
Oeuvre où la bienfaisance et la grace jumelles
Plaisent à mes regards et charment mon esprit."

So Henri Meslier, who loved the "château", described it long afterwards.

Externally the Hospital differed very little from the present school building. The northern court was unroofed and the openings in the curtain wall were unglazed; the playground sloped down unterraced to the southern wall; the art hall and its connecting bridge and west door were not to be added till 1909. Otherwise there has been no change. Internally the space was divided into different shapes and most of the existing rooms had different functions.

On the ground floor visitors entered, as now, between the two gatehouses, now the prefects' room and the armoury; but this front door was long forbidden to boys. The two gatehouses served the hospital as barber's and shoemaker's shops, the present armoury serving also, at need, as mortuary. The room facing the visitor as he came in was the dining room, occupying the space now used by room 6 and by the secretary's and janitors' rooms. Under it, entered from the playground by a sloping ramp, was the playroom. The position of the dining room determined the use of much of the ground floor. Room 5 was broken up into pantry, crockery store, butler's pantry and wine cellar—but who drank the wine is not known; room 4 was the kitchen, from which doors led into a divided room 3, divided into larder, scullery and store. The curious little porch at the eastern corner of the room was a covered space where ashes were stored before removal. Room 2 was the servants' hall. The rest of the west wing was the housekeeper's, her store, her bedroom, and, in room 1, her sitting-room. Over this west wing, with the exception of room 1, there lay a mezzanine floor, giving room for servants' bedrooms, store places for boys' Sunday clothes, and a large bathroom. A similar floor over room 5 was used to provide bedrooms for the kitchen servants.

The eastern part of the ground floor has seen fewer changes. Rooms 8 and 10 were then classrooms; room 7 was divided, the eastern part making a reception room for visitors and the western a small dining parlour for masters; the present headmaster's room was the trustees' room.

Upstairs most of the space was used as sleeping quarters. Rooms

12, 13, 14, 15, 17, 18, and 19 were boys' dormitories, spacious enough dormitories, for numbers never rose above sixty-eight in the hospital. To make supervision easier rooms 13, 14 and 15 and 17, 18 and 19 were intercommunicating—traces of the passage still remain in the cupboards in 17 and 18; and rooms 13 and 19 were subdivided to provide master's cubicles. The rest of the west wing was used as infirmary quarters, room 20 as the convalescent room, 20x as the nurses' room, 21 as the sick room and 22 as the infectious diseases segregation ward. The east wing was kept for the house governor and the trustees. The house governor had a bedroom and a sitting room made out of room 12x and the east part of room 11; the trustees used as a committee room the rest of room 11. Appropriately enough the finest room in the school was the chapel.

The sanitary arrangements upstairs were tucked away in odd corners. One "office" was in the west turret of room 11, another under the east attic stairs and the remaining two were in the spaces now used for the stairs leading up to the organ loft. Some kind of central heating was installed. A flue passed up the west side of the dining room entrance to heat the chapel and upper corridor, though even then the chapel must have been icy in winter. The other rooms were heated till the nineteen twenties by open fires, the stone hearths of which still protrude under the blackboards in most rooms. The number of fireplaces explains the ash storage space.

The general impression is of generous, even extravagant, use of room, with the whole building providing no more than three classrooms. The trustees with two good rooms did rather well and the housekeeper lived in dignity at least, though her vast sitting room was hard to keep warm. The masters fared less well. Indeed the house-governor's suite was positively cramped and the assistants' bed-sitting-rooms were mere boxes, lightly partitioned-off from the dormitories. Quite the oddest thing is the place given to the kitchen and its annexes. We are so used to finding in the great houses of the period that the kitchen is in the basement that it comes as a surprise to find it a large well-lit, south room. Here are no sunless dungeons, with stone floors worn by the hurrying feet of servants by day and cockroaches by night, no endless passages up which the same servants carry unceasingly buckets of coal and jugs of water. It is compact and sensibly arranged. The sick-rooms, too, seem more than adequate—three largish rooms for the casualties among sixty-eight boys; the space allocated is commensurate with the surgeon's salary of £50 for part-time duties which can never have been onerous.

Into the completed building in 1854 were moved those furnishings which Daniel Stewart had left to his hospital:—

" (1) My full length Picture by Raeburn
(2) The six Portrait Paintings
(3) The Painting on Copper" (It showed Brook Watson's rescue from a shark)
" (4) My House Clock
(5) My Mahogany Cloth Press
(6) The large double Press with eighteen Drawers
(7) A settee complete with two sets of covers
(8) A folding Wanescote Screen
(9) The two fine covered Mahogany Stools for Soles of Windows.
(10) The large folio Bible in two Volumes with Notes
(11) A Mahogany Night Table
(12) A Mahogany Night Box with a black Leather Top."

These remained in the Hospital till 1871 when most of them were moved into the boarding-house for foundationers set up at 10 Saxe-Coburg Place under Mrs. Hislop, to be sold in 1880 when Mrs. Hislop was dismissed and the boarding system finally ended.

Daniel Stewart's pictures came too, from Adam Longmore's house where they had been stored, to hang in the trustees' room. He had shown taste in his collection of seven portraits:—Baron Maule of the Exchequer by Allan Ramsay; Mrs. Lockhart, wife of Charles Lockhart of Lee and Carnwath, by Davidson; James, Second Duke of Atholl, by Allan Ramsay; Mary, Queen of Scots, by Jamesone after Zucchero; Patrick Lindsay, second son of the fourteenth Earl of Crawford; Baron Mure by Allan Ramsay; and Raeburn's portrait of Stewart himself.

The portraits had been a source of worry to the Trustees. Stored for a while in the Register House, then in an empty house at 21 Crosscauseway, the pictures had suffered a little from damp and light. Before Adam Longmore housed them he had to have them cleaned. Now they hang in the Merchants' Hall but the school has a copy of Raeburn's portrait of Daniel Stewart made by Tom Curr in 1953.*

The Hospital stood in ample grounds, more spacious than we

* Another copy of the portrait was made in 1905 by Charles Beatson for G. Jobson Marples, a descendant of Daniel Stewart's housekeeper, Miss Livingstone. In 1929 when Mr. Marples died the copy of the portrait was bought by the late Mr. Charles Boot, managing director of Henry Boot & Sons, Ltd., Banner Cross Hall, Sheffield. He had the features over-painted with those of his own grandfather and the portrait hung in the head offices of the firm.

STEWART'S COLLEGE FOOTBALL CLUB 1st XV., 1887-88.

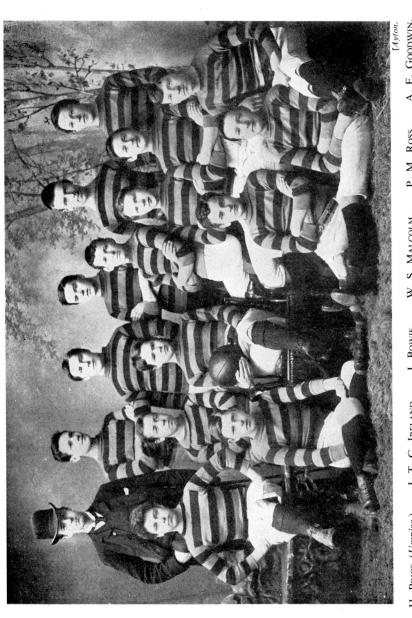

[*Ayton.*

H. Price (*Umpire.*)   J. T. C. Ireland.   J. Bowie.   W. S. Malcolm.   P. M. Ross.   A. E. Goodwin.
J. McEchern. W. Main. R. Proudfoot (*Captain*). W. P. Sangster. W. Fell. J. T. Mitchell. T. B. Paterson.
J. E. Dods.   R. Yule.   D. Allan.

have now, for some of the west part has been lost by feuing. The land was originally part of the Dean estate which was exposed for sale in 1835, in lots. The trustees bought lot 4, 11 acres, 1 rood, 26 poles (Imperial Measure), for £2000 and considered their purchase a bargain; for in more accessible parts of the town, in Bruntsfield for example, land was fetching £500 an acre. Lot 4 was bounded on three sides by its present limits, but on the west it stretched to Queensferry Terrace, the "old Queensferry Road" of those days, a miry track which was used after 1870 by those day-boys who used to come along it from Haymarket to school. Until 1848 the land was let, as arable, to a neighbouring farmer.

After the hospital building was finished the grounds remained a source of worry to the Trustees. A kitchen garden brought in some vegetables, there was a bowling green—presumably for the masters—the boys had the clinker-covered south playground, but the rest was untidy, with huge approaches where weeds flourished. In 1862 the Merchant Company took expert opinion of Lawson and Son, the Nurserymen, but for some reason did not follow most of the advice. The wide entrance drive, now divided by a strip of turf and the war memorial, the experts wanted to divide by a row of chestnuts—they would be fine now in May—underplanted with Irish yews and gentians; the present tennis courts they wanted to cultivate for two years, resow with fine grass, and keep short with sheep; the front terrace, they thought, should hold one or two Wellingtonias or cedars. One, at least, of their recommendations was carried out—the row of trees along the back entrance, the goals of so many games, was planted.

In 1872 another attempt was made to rid the governors of the expense of the upkeep of the grounds. They leased to Hunter, their gardener, everything except the front lawns and the playground, to cultivate as a market garden, while he, in return for the lodge and £5 a year, undertook to keep the front lawns trim. This system lasted till 1879 when fresh plans were made. Hunter again entered the service of the school as gardener; and his market-garden became a nursery where young trees were grown to restock the various Merchant Company estates—Colinton, Balbardie, etc. This new plan, in turn, had a short life. The west part of the grounds were leased to Mr. Hill to add as garden to his existing feu of Dean Park House; the rest was committed to a firm of nurserymen to look after; and preparations—plans A and B—were made to feu all the rest of the ground except open spaces immediately in front of and behind the school.

This feuing was no new thing. The first encroachment on the land was made in 1864 when the house governor was given leave to marry and had a new house built for him in the corner between Queensferry Road and Queensferry Terrace, the house called now the "Corner House" and then "Stewart Villa."* Between 1873 and 1879 the rest of the ground now occupied by houses was feued. It was an unfortunate but well-meant decision. At a time when organised games were of so little importance the governors decided that the ground needed for an enclosed hospital was too great, and too expensive in upkeep, for a day school; and they had constantly to think of increasing their revenues if fees were to be kept down.

* The house was disposed of when Mr. King died, and not till this year (when No. 14 Ravelston Dykes was bought) has the Headmaster had an official house.

THE HOSPITAL II

ARLY in 1855 the first fifty boys, chosen out of seventy-six applicants, began their hospital life, half on 30th January, half on 6th February. They found in it the security, the warmth, the food, as well as the learning that many of them lacked outside; for while it is likely that the ornate new building rising among the fields with raw, ungravelled walks leading to it would appear to most of them a prison and a palace, their guardians or surviving parents must have seen it with other eyes. A large number of the boys had lost one parent, or both; many, to judge by the Headmaster's reports, can have had little schooling. Besides, the year was unsettled. It is worth remembering that these boys came into the hospital in war time, that Britain and Russia were at war. During the autumn news had come from the Crimea, news of the Alma and of the 93rd's action at Balaclava, and from the Baltic where Cronstadt had been attempted. At home the war brought scarcity, high prices and unemployment, with 6d. a day offered as unemployed pay in Edinburgh. Two of the boys must have been very conscious of the nearness of the war: John Handyside had lost his mother, and his father, a colour-sergeant of the Royal Artillery was "at present before Sebastopol"; Mackenzie Sinclair, a fatherless boy, had an absent mother, a nurse "at present with Miss Nightingale in the 'East'."

We know a good deal about this first fifty. A "Register of Boys admitted into Daniel Stewart's Hospital" was kept, not a soulless waste of noughts and crosses, but a decent large ledger, bound in calf, with full entries in a lovely hand. It gives us their names, their ages, their fathers' occupations and names, their mothers' addresses, the "cautioners" for each, a note of their attainments when they came in, and, twice, on their attainments and future occupations when they left. It gives us, too, their numbers, their personal numbers. By some hideous lack of imagination hospitallers were known rather by number than by name, so that, twenty years after, they could greet one another: "Hallo, 47. You remember me, 38?" The same system seems to have been used at Heriot's where the numbers are still engraved in the flagstones.

There were only three Stewarts and two Macfarlanes in the first fifty, surprisingly few. The other names—Wilson, Forrest, Fraser, Taylor, Mowat, Sinclair and the like—are almost all names still on the register. Thirty-four were fatherless, and six others may have been; at least there are six entries which say of the fathers "at present supposed to be residing in London," "a native of Ireland: deserted his family," or "in Australia." The "cautioners" ranged from ministers of religion, such as the Reverend Dr. Muir of St. Stephen's to Helen and Euphemia Bisset, cooks in "good" families, who sponsored their orphaned nephew.

The fathers' occupations give us some idea of the boys' backgrounds. Their homes were lowly enough when their fathers were with them; the forty who had lost their fathers must have seen even their little worlds breaking up. Most came from labouring or artisan families: six were sons of masons or other building craftsmen, five of porters, two of printers—one of these, Sergeant Stewart of the Grenadiers, had fought at Waterloo—three of railwaymen, and two of tailors. The rest ranged through the ranks of small shop-keepers and various humble occupations, with a dead Writer at one end of the social scale and a "Pauper in the Parish of Ayr" at the other. It was rather a pathetic collection of little boys, their ages running from seven to ten, who came in. Most had suffered from some family misfortune and some found the past hard to slough: it is certainly noticeable that there was at first trouble with bed-wetting in the dormitories and some of the offenders had to be removed to the convalescent room.

Intelligence tests were mercifully unknown; the boys' attainments were tested mainly by reading, especially from the "Irish book," a graded primer. Against each name is set the part of the "Irish book" he could manage—when he could manage any of it —and occasionally a word about his ignorance of grammar or arithmetic. John Middleton, the son of a dead exciseman "could read the 4th Irish book; knew nothing of Grammar and little of Arithmetic." He was almost ten. But, in spite of his shortcomings, he was among the most proficient. The average boy found the second Irish book difficult enough, and many had not yet approached the first: John Stewart, a shoemaker's son "knew the Alphabet, could not, however, distinguish 'p' from 'q' " and George Thomson had the same difficulty, with "v" and "y" as added bothers. Worse, Robert Hunter, at seven and a half "when admitted could not repeat the alphabet" and was exceedingly stupid. What was made of him is not said, unfortunately, but we see that two, at least, the two eldest, Thomas Chisholm and John Middleton, left with some learning: Chisholm "could read Virgil" and Middleton "could read Virgil and Xenophon." The one went as clerk to a shipping office, the other to be a pupil teacher in Manchester.

The register continued until 1903, when an inquiry into the

organisation of the Merchant Company schools was held, and much unnecessary clerking was stopped. After 1870 it remained a register of foundationers, but the early enthusiasm was lost and the entries become less and less informative, recording, finally, little more than the boy's name and age. Yet a little can be gleaned from it. In 1857 the numbers were increased by fourteen, and were to range from sixty to seventy for the next thirteen years. In other words the classes were very small for the 1860's, neither of the two masters having more than thirty-five boys.

The little community comes to life for us in 1868. It was the time when the Merchant Company was questioning the value of the hospitals and was seeking outside opinions. The fullest and most valuable of these reports was that of Simon S. Laurie, an intelligent and sensible observer, although later a professor of Education. His report was based on five visits, each of at least three hours; on a careful examination of the classes; and on enlightened snooping. He shows the boys rising at six on summer mornings (at seven in winter time) and following a rigid timetable till nine at night. They began with three-quarters of an hour for washing and dressing, a quarter of an hour in chapel and an hour for play. Breakfast at eight was followed by school from nine till twelve, with a dinner interval of an hour and three-quarters and afternoon school till half-past five. At four there was a short break for the afternoon piece. After tea the hour from six to seven was used for prep with an hour and a half for supper (that would not take long) and play, before evening chapel and bed. Play in winter was difficult; classrooms were used, and damaged.

Sunday was equally rigorous for those who stayed in hospital. The day began with three-quarters of an hour prep. After two hours in church—the newly built Dean Church, where sittings had been taken—in the morning, and an hour and three-quarters there in the afternoon, the day ended with an hour's religious instruction under classmasters. Sunday must have schooled them in patient sitting at least.

Lack of animal spirits helped to keep them quiet. Laurie was struck by it and wrote, "While the boys look healthy, they have not that expression of super-abundant vigour which looks out of the faces of boys in the High School or Edinburgh Academy." His comment appears almost unnecessary when we read his account of their food. Breakfast was of porridge and sweet milk (the adjective matters: poor people used skim milk), the afternoon piece of butterless bread, and supper of bread and milk. The dinners varied: Sunday's was rice pudding, bread and milk; Monday's was pea-soup, bread and potatoes; Tuesday's and Friday's included both soup and meat; and Saturday's was stew with bread and potatoes. There is no entry for Wednesday; it may have been a lean day. The food was wholesome enough, except the bread, which was condemned as impure in 1863, but not likely to lead to riotous behaviour from excess of protein.

The teaching staff was small, never more than three resident masters including the house-governor who taught the senior classes, with visiting masters for drawing, singing, instrumental music—there was a hospital band—and dancing. Dancing began after the Merchant Company took over the hospital and roused debate, one of the Assistants saying, "Hitherto the boys of the Hospital, thanks to the excellent training of Mr. Ogilvie . . . have *not* been taught to regard themselves as Gentlemen." The Rev. Hugh Niven, of the Chapel of Ease at Gartmore, was the first house-governor but his stay was short. He left to become a minister in Canada, leaving no impression on the Hospital. (Mr. Niven became minister of Saltfeet and Binbrook in the province of Ontario in 1857.) In June 1856, from the Parochial School at Turriff, came George Ogilvie, M.A. to begin his long work in Edinburgh, and put the hospital firmly on its feet, for £150 a year. His domestic staff was considerable: W. Burn Murdoch was surgeon at £50 a year; Miss Rochead was matron till 1871; there was a gardener—McLennan, who will appear later, two warders, a nurse, three laundry maids, a tablemaid, two ward maids, and a cook at £12 a year.

The masters' days were not easy. Each one took his class through all the subjects of the course, and each class was divided into at least two sections. Certainly the number in each class was small, but for the junior master the day had twenty-four hours; he slept in the boys' ward. There is not space to look at all the classes and their work; the upper division of eighteen boys, the thirteen and fourteen year olds taught by Ogilvie must serve as sample. Their daily timetable gave half an hour to French and to writing, an hour to the English subjects and to Latin, two hours to arithmetic, and an hour to singing or to drawing. (The Greek of the early days had disappeared by 1868.) In Latin, *Caesar* and *Virgil* were read, in French, *Paul et Virginie* and, in English, *Marmion*. The abler mathematicians had mastered Euclid's first two books and in algebra had reached simple equations. Of the work generally, Laurie could say that it would stand comparison with what was done in the Academy or High School by boys of the same age, and Ogilvie, writing half a century later to one of the first entrants, could say, "It is interesting to me to recall to your remembrance the fact that you undertook to conjugate all irregular Latin verbs, and that you made only one mistake." Boys such as Adamson, too, went straight from hospital to University and from 1866 to 1869 hospital boys were first each year in the University Local Examinations.

From the Sederunt Books of the original trustees, and from the Minute Books of the governors after 1860 something can be learned about the daily economy of the hospital and about the inmates. The contractors' prices are revealing: boots cost 7s. or 8s. a pair, socks 14s. 6d. to 19s. 6d. a dozen; the tweed cloth of everyday wear was 4s. 6d. a yard and the tailoring of a suit (with future repairs) was £1, 9s. 9d.; superfine blue cloth (for Sunday wear, perhaps) was dearer, 11s. 6d. a yard; milk was 10½d. a gallon and boiling meat 6s. 5d. a stone. Assistant masters could be had for £60 with their board. The figures enable us to see the real value of the endowment.

Some minor discords and upsets marred these serene years. Boys slid down banisters and one, Stewart, fell over, involving the trustees in the expense of the oak studs which still prevent us. Two others showed their opinion of the place by repeatedly running off to sea (or rather towards the sea, for they were unsuccessful) until they were expelled. Perhaps they were not our type anyway. "Neither of the boys were (*sic*) desirable inmates of the Institution. X being a stupid, obstinate, intractable boy, and Y, though of good abilities, cunning and imbued with bad principles which it seemed impossible to eradicate, as well as extremely dirty in his habits." The gatekeeper, too, was unsatisfactory. He was "indolent, careless and indifferent," and his language was not above censure. On St. Andrew's day in 1861 the visiting governors had to report, "On this occasion an opportunity was taken to speak to the party, MacLennan, the gatekeeper, as to his removal to make way for the occupancy of the New Gardener, but on introducing the circumstance we were met with such an uncourteous style of language as to preclude further communication." MacLennan's irritation may have been caused in part by the governors' refusal to admit his son to the foundation. He left soon after and the admirable Hunter succeeded him. Once, in 1862, the Christmas holiday was delayed till March because of the smallpox epidemic in Edinburgh.

But these are little things: the governors could reasonably be satisfied with their stewardship for they provided, as well as the meal, the trifles that sweetened it. They bought cricket gear in 1862; they rewarded the duxes with a silver medal each year; they spent £5 or so most years on books; they took the boys off each summer on jaunts to the country—to Peebles, or Stirling, or Dalmeny; they entertained the former hospitallers at school in 1866 (the first F.P. reunion) on 18th May; and when the first ten boys left in 1859 they paid the apprenticeship fees of those who wished to be apprenticed to a trade. The reward for their enlightened work was the hospitaller, the typical boy. In 1865 David Dickson, a Visitor, later to be Master of the Merchant Company, wrote "I was struck to-day by again observing distinctly the frank, open look of the boys here—so unlike the old, well-known "smorrl" or *scowl* of the Hospital boys." From their ranks some distinguished men were to come: Henry Kerr Rutherford who came in 1855, the son of a dead hosier, trained as a civil engineer before going to Ceylon where he pioneered tea-growing; Robert Adamson who became professor of Logic in Glasgow University; or Young J. Pentland who was an Assistant of the Merchant Company between 1916 and 1919.

But the hospital system was not popular. The Argyll Commission on Scottish Education in 1868 reported unfavourably on it, quoting costs to show how extravagant it was: Stewart's spent £47, 5s. per boy, Watson's £64 per boy, and the Merchant Maiden Hospital £47 per girl. These were compared with costs in Gillespie's Free School where 16s. paid for the education of a boy and in Hutcheson's, where £2, 10s. sufficed, to elicit the mild comment: "It appears to us, therefore, that the cost of education in hospitals is larger than it ought to be." A leading article in *The Scotsman*, 29th July, 1868, went further: "The sum annually expended in the Hospitals of Edinburgh is larger than the total assessment for the maintenance of the parochial schools of Scotland, and more than half the expenditure of the Privy Council on schools of all kinds in the northern part of the kingdom, including the payments necessary for the training of masters and mistresses." Laurie too, had been unfriendly to the system, although impressed by Stewart's. His final summing up was, "I do not think the system a wholesome one, either morally or intellectually." It appears that the system of monastic education, which produced the leaders of England for a century when the boys came from wealthy families and were allowed a good deal of self-government, produced, when the boys came from poor homes and were handled in a different way "a painful monotony of look and air . . . the destruction of personality." The reforms he proposed would, if carried out, have condemned us and Watson's to exist as mere preparatory schools and boarding houses for the Royal High School. "There is only one way of removing them (the evils of the hospital system) and of giving full effect to the benevolent intentions of the founders of these Institutions: and *this is by converting the Houses into Boarding Establishments and sending the boys for their instruction to the High School, or some similar establishment.* Sections 1 and 11, composed of boys under ten, may be taught as at present in the hospital and there made ready for the first class in the High School."

The Merchant Company wisely found a better cure for the evils of the hospital system, applying to all their hospitals the remedy Laurie had suggested for the Merchant Maiden Hospital, and turning them into feepaying day schools where foundationers survived as a minority of the boys. In September 1870 the Hospital became the Daniel Stewart's Institution or Day School.

ADMINISTRATION

OR its first six years the hospital was governed in terms of Daniel Stewart's Will, by his co-opted trustees—John Burn Murdoch of Gartencaber, John Burn Murdoch, Junior, and Adam Chalmers Longmore of the Exchequer, with John A. Longmore as clerk and treasurer. On 1st February 1860 the Merchant Company was to take over, under the Will. But the Company was prudent and looked sharply at the gift horse before accepting it, in spite of the £300 promised by Daniel Stewart. In 1859 a Report on the hospital by the Master, Treasurer and Assistants was published, showing that they had made a careful examination of the Hospital and its endowments, and that they found both satisfactory. Indeed the endowments had increased from the £18,000 of 1814 to some £81,000 with a surplus of income over expenditure of £1,100, but they were careful to note that the rents from the shops and houses in the Old Town were likely to fall soon as the Old Town decayed. On their report the Company, on 4th April 1859, in the Merchants' Hall in Hunter Square, agreed that the Master, Treasurer and Assistants should accept the burden of government of the hospital. For the next ten years it was ruled by them, and they remained Governors after the change to a day school in 1870, the actual administration being divided between a Standing Committee, an Education Committee and the Monthly Visitors—two of the Governors each month undertaking the task of visiting and inspecting, as they still do.

The Hospital did not come under the Merchant Company, as a company. Counsel's opinion had been taken in 1859 whether the Company could legally undertake the management and whether it needed to have its powers confirmed by statute or charter. The Solicitor-General pointed out that the Will had given the governorship to the Master, Treasurer and Assistants only, and recommended that their authority be made statutory. For convenience we may use the term "Merchant Company" when speaking of the Governors. A private Act of Parliament therefore, of 6th August 1860 authorised the transfer and gave the new Governors increased powers, both to dispose of the property in the Old Town which Daniel Stewart had reserved and to invest in landed property. For Daniel Stewart had laid down that his funds should be invested in securities, and counsel in 1845 had ruled that the trustees would be acting *ultra vires* in purchasing estates. Immediately the Act was passed the Governors began to look for a suitable estate: this was still the age of high farming and the return from land seemed both considerable and secure. Longhaven, an estate marching with Peterhead, another Merchant Company estate, was first considered, but not bought. A nearer one was bought in 1861—Balbardie estate near Bathgate of 854 acres. The price, £48,000 was high, but the income was estimated at £2,000 and there was the certainty that this could be increased: the leases of four of the farms were soon to expire and they could be renewed at higher rents; two hundred acres lying waterlogged could be drained and made into another farm; the feu duties—there were two hundred and sixty-seven vassals—extended over all Bathgate, and Bathgate was rapidly expanding; there was a distillery (Glenmavis), a lime works, a quarry, and coal and ironstone workings on the land. In short, it appeared a very promising investment, and was to prove so. The governors took over the duties of the lairds of Balbardie and were not ungenerous benefactors of the town of Bathgate. They are still represented on the West Lothian Educational Trust.

So far we have spoken of the Hospital as if it were alone of its kind. It may be worth saying that Daniel Stewart had added another to the many hospitals already existing, or about to exist in Scotland—Robert Gordon's, Morgan's, Heriot's, Mary Erskine's and others were already in being; and Sir William Fettes in 1836 had left his money to found another. But by the 1860's the climate of opinion was against the system, and the Merchant Company set an example to the others in changing the purpose of the endowments under their care, urging the Lord Advocate to introduce permissive legislation. The Endowed Institutions (Scotland) Act of 1869 gave them freedom to act, to apply to the Secretary of the Home Department for a provisional order that would enable them to alter the terms of the trust deeds of their foundations, to improve their educational usefulness. This Order was applied for, granted, and approved by Parliament in 1870. It gave the Merchant Company the right to convert Daniel Stewart's and Mary Erskine's Hospitals into feepaying day schools, to turn George Watson's into a double day school for boys and girls and to unite the funds of James Gillespie's foundation to provide a bigger elementary school. At the same time Bathgate Academy, which had the Master as one of its Governors, also obtained permission to amend its trust deed.

The Order made greater changes than the mere conversion to a day school. The Merchant Company was authorised to set up a new system of government for its schools. The Merchant Company

Hospitals Board, consisting of the Master, Treasurer and the Conveners of the Education Committee of each Hospital was to form a consulting body with powers to make recommendations to the governors of each Hospital. The name was changed from Daniel Stewart's Hospital to Daniel Stewart's Institution—a name used until 1888, officially, though it was called "College" after 1880, and foundationers were removed from the building. The Order made sure that the new Institution would not follow the too common Scottish practice in higher schools, where the headmaster ruled as *primus inter pares*. It laid down that "all the teachers and other persons under him shall be appointed by and hold their office at his pleasure." It was a wise decision and we have been fortunate, in another sense, in keeping the substance of it: teachers are still appointed on the recommendations of the Headmaster to the Board; we have been in the main kept free of men appointed after committee canvassing. Day boys, as many as could be accommodated, were to be admitted at moderate fees, £2 a quarter, after passing an examination suitable to their years. They were to be in no way inferior to foundationers in standing: they were eligible for bursaries to meet the cost of tuition; they could compete equally for the university bursaries of £25 a year now made available from the Hospital funds; and they could themselves be elected foundationers.

There were greater changes in the foundation. The Argyll Commission of 1868 had said of bursaries in general: "The conditions of poverty attached to most of the bursaries is of very doubtful utility. It seems, at first sight, wise and considerate, but it would greatly increase the good done by the bursaries, and the value attached to them, if this condition were repealed. Bursaries should be the prizes of merit, and poor students, we may be sure, would win their fair share of them in open competition." This expresses the spirit of the age and obviously the framers of the Order were influenced by it. Stewarts and MacFarlanes no longer had any preference, and the Governors could apply more exacting tests for admission than good health and parental poverty. "In selecting out of the applicants those who shall be admitted regard shall be had by the Governors to the merits and attainments of each applicant as tested by the examination . . . and the Governors shall have power to place upon the Foundation any scholar whose merits and attainments, as tested by examination, are such as to entitle him to that privilege." The number of foundationers was to be reduced to forty and the field of choice narrowed, "One half at least of the foundationers for the time being shall be elected by competitive examination from the day scholars of Daniel Stewart's

GYMNASTICS, 1920's.

GYMNASTICS, 1950's.

Hospital, George Watson's Hospital and James Gillespie's Schools."
In 1876 seven foundationers were chosen, three by merit and four
by favour. But it is noticeable that even the four chosen by favour
distinguished themselves in the examination which all the applicants
had to sit. The arrangement by which Watson's boys could share
half our foundations seldom worked to our advantage. Too often
they were allowed to remain at Watson's while drawing a stipend
from Stewart's funds. For the Order had provided that Watson's
should be the leading Merchant Company school for boys. "The
education to be provided in Daniel Stewart's Schools (the governors
were authorised to set up more than one school) shall be of a
more advanced character than that in James Gillespie's Schools,
and the education to be provided in George Watson's Schools
shall be of a more advanced character than that in Daniel Stewart's
Schools." Ogilvie, who had made so much of Daniel Stewart's
Hospital was transferred to Watson's as the first Headmaster of
the day school.

Room had to be found outside the school building for those
foundationers who could not live at home; at first they were boarded
in Saxe-Coburg Place in a house run by Miss Rochead till her
retirement in 1871. The Governors clothed them and paid for
their board. The bill for boots must have been heavy: foundationers made their way to school in a body, playing football with
tins as they went. After Miss Rochead's retirement, Mrs. Hislop
was appointed matron to run the boarding-house and supervise
foundationers boarded privately, being careful to see that her own
boarders were regular in their attendance at St. Bernard's Church.
The house in Saxe-Coburg Place was given up in 1873 but Mrs.
Hislop continued as matron, running a house at 13 Hope Street
where three foundationers boarded, and supervising the others
till 1880, when the furnishings of the house, many brought from the
Hospital, were sold.

The care of the school was shared among the Governors. Committees—Finance, Education, Estates and Visiting—were formed
to deal with the routine things, and we can judge of their care from
the Visitors' Book and Minute Books. The Visitors' Book records
the visits of the monthly visitors and usually some comment shows
that the visit was more than a formality. The Minute Books are
even more revealing. Their pages show the endless pains taken
by the governors over all the details of the management of the
school. They used their funds with generosity as well as prudence
to help F.P.s in many ways. Herbert Down, an apprentice phar-
macist, applied for a grant to help his studies, and was given
£6, 10s. a year; John Turner, an old foundationer in ill-health, had

a country holiday arranged and paid for; John Parker, a foundationer who died, had his funeral paid for; even Mrs. Hislop's son had a grant to pay his emigration expenses; and many of the unsuccessful applicants for foundations received a year's free education. The earthen path which lay between the north boundary and Queensferry Road was used by the public for horse-exercise, to the danger of the boys; the minutes record, year by year from 1875 till 1892, the governors' correspondence with the Town Council and Chief Constable until they succeeded in having the stretch in front of the gate paved to stop galloping. They advertised the school widely, having nineteen thousand prospectuses printed in 1876 for distribution among the ten-pound householders. In 1877 they relaid the playground, covering the original clinkers with rolled gravel; they put up the playsheds in 1891 and in the following year gave the playground its present form by levelling it and building the retaining parapet. Innumerable other examples could be cited. Perhaps none is more revealing than the report they required, quarterly and annually, from the headmaster, a detailed report, with a list of books used as a supplement; and the care they gave to the scrutiny of each report.

The Order of 1870 remained in force till 1888. The 1882 Educational Endowments (Scotland) Act, designed to reorganise all endowments made before 1872, had set up a commission of seven members to make and approve new schemes. This commission under the chairmanship of Lord Balfour and Burleigh was meticulous in its long labours and, over all Scotland, extended the usefulness of endowments, carrying out more fully the founders' intentions, having regard to the altered circumstances of the times. For Stewart's a new Scheme was approved by the Queen, 17th November, 1888, modifying considerably the terms of the 1878 Order. The status within the Merchant Company hierarchy was altered: we acquired educational parity with Watson's and retained educational superiority over Gillespie's. The Governors were given freedom to change the name from Institution to whatever they liked. The benefits formerly shared by Watson's boys were taken from them: the 1870 Order had laid down that half the foundationers should be chosen from the three boys' schools; the 1888 Scheme prescribed that half should come from Stewart's only. But the flow of good boys from Gillespie's was to continue: "The Governors shall also have power not to charge or require payment of tuition fees of any bursars transferred by the Governors of James Gillespie's schools to attend as pupils of Daniel Stewart's Schools."

There is another administrative change in the 1888 Scheme: the Scotch Education Department made its appearance: "The schools shall be periodically inspected in such manner as the Scotch Education Department shall from time to time prescribe." Already the benevolent octopus, which had begun its separate life in 1885 under Sir Henry Craik, was reaching out, as the extracts show, over both teaching and finance, The first casualty was the Bathgate Agricultural Association: the annual subscription of two guineas paid by the Governors as lairds of Balbardie was disallowed.

So far each of the Merchant Company schools had grown in isolation. Some small administration unity had been given by the Merchant Company Hospitals Board of 1870 and by the Treasurers' Committee of 1881. This was made up of the Master, the Treasurer, the honorary treasurers of each of the governing boards, and one other member of each governing board, and had the general duty of supervising the whole income and expenditure of the Merchant Company trusts. Both these bodies were abolished in 1895 by the Edinburgh Merchant Company Endowments Act, which set up in their place the Merchant Company Endowments Board of fourteen members under the chairmanship of the Master. The members were elected by the Boards of Governors of the schools; two were to be ministers; four were to be town councillors (the other schools had such people on their governing bodies). The new Board had considerable powers over each of the separate governing bodies: it was yearly to receive all surplus revenue from each and so create a central fund to be used partly to make up deficits in any of the separate accounts, partly to create a reserve fund to meet extraordinary expenditure on buildings and partly to make contributions to a superannuation fund for teachers. It meant, in fact, that the wealthier schools were to help their poorer relations. In its fourteen years of life the Central Fund was to accumulate £13,000.

The duties of the Board entailed others which lessened farther the powers of the separate governing bodies. It was to regulate the fees in each school, to fix the length of the sessions, to decide the amount to be spent on prizes, to appoint examiners, and the like. Centralisation had begun.

It was completed in December 1909 by the Edinburgh Merchant Company Endowments Order. This Act cancelled both the Order of 1870 and the 1888 Scheme, dissolving both the separate governing bodies and the 1895 Board. It replaced them by an Education Board of twenty-four members—the Master, Treasurer and twelve Assistants; the Lord Provost and four other councillors; two ministers of the Edinburgh presbytery; and three co-opted members —a representative board with adequate representation of the Merchant Company. With the separate governing bodies the separate endowments vanished: both the endowments and the Central Fund of 1895 were amalgamated to form one common endowment to be used for the benefit of the *four* schools under the care of the Education Board. Gillespie's was given up; the buildings and furnishings were to be sold and the proceeds, with the capitalised endowment, paid to the Education Board. As in the past most of the work was delegated to committees, finance and audit, education, estates, and superannuation.

The new Order was retrograde in dealing with foundations. The old regulations of 1870 which had made possible the election of foundationers by merit were cancelled, and the terms for admission to the foundation—now limited to twenty boys—were to be those in force in 1854. Educationally no more could be required of the candidate than that he should pass an entrance examination suitable to his age. It is on paper closer to the founder's intention, but he had not envisaged a society of free education and state care for the young. The other system had made it possible to have such men as Hugh Martin or Sir Gordon Lethem as foundationers. It was worth while competing for a foundation place: the reward was free education and £21 paid in golden money. We need merely notice the way in which year by year very able boys are attracted to other schools by scholarships to regret that after 1909 none of our places was competitive. Certainly the Board was empowered to help able boys in other ways—by offering school attendance scholarships giving free tuition, and school bursaries giving free tuition and a small yearly allowance, one hundred and fifty scholarships and one hundred bursaries among the four schools. The Board was also permitted to award university bursaries, modern language scholarships, and travelling scholarships. In short they were permitted to use part of their funds to reward ability and effort among the pupils of the schools, as well as provide for the foundationers. The final reform—'change' is a better word—was made in 1931, and approved by the Earl of Elgin's committee, a committee set up by the 1928 Education Endowments (Scotland) Act. They were not drastic changes: the Education Board was increased to twenty-eight members by adding another three co-opted members and another town councillor, at the same time making it possible for members of the Education Committee of the Town Council to be of the five; school bursaries were retained (after a strong protest by the Merchant Company at the Elgin Committee's proposal to abolish them). but restricted in duration to one year and in amount to £500 a year for the four schools;

In one way the Committee was too mindful of its commission.

Its report said: "Under section 3 of the Act we are enjoined in reorganising endowments to have a special regard to the spirit of the intention of the founder." The members evidently considered that the intention of the founder was to provide for foundationers, for they insisted that the 1909 maximum of twenty foundationers should become an irreducible minimum.

After the abolition of the separate governing bodies, vice-conveners were appointed for each school for a yearly term of office which is normally extended to a second year. Their task is to act as the liaison officer between schools and the Board but most have been much more than that. Advisers, benefactors, schemers sometimes, they seem to have identified themselves wholly with the school and we have gained immensely from the services of men who have distinguished themselves in the world of commerce or industry, and have brought their knowledge of larger affairs to our little world.

No other changes worth noticing have been made to the ruling of the school. The Committee on Educational Endowments in Scotland looked at us in 1950, noted how few independent schools remained in Scotland, and passed on with this comment, which may stand as the peroration: "We are satisfied that as long as these schools maintain the individual characteristics and worthy traditions which have long been theirs and play their part in association with normal public provision in meeting the educational needs of the community, even though they have to depend on substantial assistance from public funds to do so, it would be a disservice to the Scottish Educational system to deprive it of the variety and quality they provide."

The school still has its twenty foundationers, though their identity is not revealed. That some are grateful is evidenced by the fact that one recently left a cheque for £1,000 at the end of his visit to the Secretary of the Merchant Company in gratitude for the help that his brother and he had received at school and in the hope—which will not be disappointed—that "some other poor kid" might profit from the gift.

THE INSTITUTION

HE new day school, Stewart's Institution, filled up slowly enough. At first the hospital buildings were too large for the numbers, and glass-panelled doors were fitted to divide the unused west wing and chapel from the rest of the school. But it soon became a living community under Mr. King, where the Bawsers, Chingies, Gubbies and Puddens were taught by Bandy, Hippletaekick and by others less kindly remembered. "One of the masters, who shall be nameless, gained nothing but hate and ill-will. His classroom was known as the "slaughterhouse" He doubtless called himself a good disciplinarian. By 1878 there were thirteen masters, specialising up to a point, with two masters to teach writing and drawing, and M. Martin to teach French.

Among the early entrants were several who were to distinguish themselves in various ways in later life. Francis Grant, a future Lyon King at Arms, came in 1871. With him at school were Samuel Rutherford MacPhail, later to distinguish himself as a specialist in mental diseases and as a Celtic enthusiast (the two studies are not necessarily connected) and Robert Innes-Smith whose *History of the English-speaking Students of Medicine at the University of Leyden* is a valuable addition to the too scanty libraries of works on the history of medicine and on the Scots in the Low Countries. H. Bonar Stuart, too, was here in 1874, before travelling far to build railways round Stalingrad and in the Caucasus, even thinking of doubling the Trans-Siberian railway. Here, too, was David J. Galloway, who qualified in medicine before going to Malaya where he rose to the dignity of Knighthood as a member of the governing council. Two of these boys, Allan R. Yule, now the doyen of Scottish C.A.'s, who came at nine years old in September 1870 and J. W. S. Wilson, who came into school from the country in October 1877, have very accurate memories of their school days. Allan Yule's memories are very clear about what happened outside the classroom though he was a creditable pupil in class. He recalls the long foot-journey to school through muddy roads, to the back gate, for boys were forbidden to use the front; the visiting baker who sold buns and baps through a ground floor window to a jostle of boys in the playground; and the playground itself, clinker-covered, with goal posts at each end where rugby was played with our halves called quarter-backs, and our three-quarters called halves. He recalls, too, a few of the masters—

Mr. Wood who taught Mathematics and came sometimes to kick a ball, and Mr. Robb, the English master, whom all seem to have liked. A steady stream of Gillespie's bursars had begun to flow to us, among them, in the seventies, Allardyce and Easton, the one to become a Professor of Stanford University, the other an antique dealer. James Rousseau, formidable as a footballer, was here, too, who was later to become Warden of Tobago. Our nearest rivals were the boys of Collegiate School—a Charlotte Square School now dead—whose field lay on the south side of Ravelston Dykes opposite the back gate. Edinburgh Institution, now Melville College, played to the east of us on the site of the present cemetery. The long way home for most of the boys lay through Dean Village, where the crossing of the mill-lade was the place for fights with the village boys; for others, especially for those coming by train to Haymarket, the miry road was made interesting by the sight of St. Mary's Cathedral being built.

Even in those days we played rugby, inspired probably by the Academy team. It was a spontaneous growth, the game chosen by the boys for themselves, with no encouragement from masters or from outside, with understandable discouragement in fact. For, as Allan Yule recalled, the playground was clinker-covered with a thin scattering of grass on the east, sloping, unterraced towards the school. Grazes and worse injuries were common. On the north side this rugby pitch was bounded by a thorn hedge, roughly where the technical department now is, backed by "the plants" a little thicket which ran down to Queensferry Road. The touch-line ran within a foot or so of this hedge and gave scope for gamesmanship; opposing wing half-backs learned to dread the tackle into touch. Not that many opponents visited us. Heriot's were brave enough to face it, but the Academy boys—who called us "cads" and fought with us along the Water of Leith—declined. On their own ground we scored a famous victory over Collegiate in 1877 when Rousseau scored the winning try.

These were games, and no more. No one yet hinted that they had educational value, nor that the prestige of the school was in any way tied to success at football. For long Mr. Massie was the only master who attended matches, not as touch-judge or referee, but simply because he liked watching football. "Windy Ravelston" was still part of Dean Farm, an annual plague to the Headmaster when the Hallows Fair was held there—an even greater temptation to kipping than Dean Village with its mills where one well-disposed miller sometimes gave handfuls of groats to the idle who found long summer afternoons in the valley more exciting than writing-room labours under Mr. Williamson.

Fees were low—£2 a quarter in 1874; hot lunches were served to supplement the baker's baps; holidays were generous—in 1876 26th October was a fast day, Christmas holidays were from 22nd December till 3rd January, Good Friday was a holiday, the Easter holidays were from 25th April till 7th May, 24th May was a holiday, the Queen's birthday of the rhyme, and the long vacation ran gloriously from 24th July till 2nd October, about fourteen weeks in all; the school was widely advertised; but in spite of all this numbers were slow to rise during the first decade.

There were about three hundred boys in 1870. By 1881 there were three hundred and twelve. Thereafter the increase was rapid —four hundred and thirty-nine in 1882, five hundred and sixty-nine in 1883, eight hundred and ninety, the greatest number as yet, in 1890 the majority leaving at fifteen or sixteen. Inside, though reports differ about this, discipline seems to have been poor; outside the classrooms it was firm; Isaac Grossett, "Sodger Jock" or "Perkins," had brought military ways from the 92nd Highlanders and his voice and whistle brooked no denial, whether the malefactor dared to climb the boundary wall in search of a lost ball, or to venture on the front lawns. For these had been let in 1882 first to the Dean Lawn Tennis Club then to the Queen Street School.

J. W. S. Wilson gives a lively picture of day-to-day life in school in 1878: "The classroom was known as number 7 and was one stair up in the east end of the school with a window looking east. There were three forms which held ten boys each with the backs to the north wall of the room. There were four or five new boys and we were all put to sit on the form at the window in alphabetical order and so I sat at the foot of the class. The boys only got up and down on the three forms.

"The teacher was a Mr. Lowe, a very nice man, who taught all subjects in Room 7 except writing and drawing, for both of which subjects we were sent downstairs to the large room situated over the 'Dungeons' to the back. The other new boys like myself knew nothing of Latin or French so that for these two subjects we were sent downstairs to the class below which was revising their Latin and beginning to learn French. After a few months we were brought back into our own class for these subjects and went on with the class.

"After the second quarterly exam I scored sufficiently high to be put in the back or top form and remained in it to the end of the session. . . .

"Two incidents, one the very first week occurred in which I was concerned. I had never seen the game of 'Rugby'. I looked on for two days watching the class playing. Charles Duggan, a nice, friendly boy, asked me to join the class rugby club and told me what the subscription was. In all it was only 2/-, I think, but I had a job getting it from my mother, as she said I would only get my legs broken. However, my father thought I would have to be like the rest of the boys and he was promptly told that he was worse than me, and so I paid my subscription. There was an old boy in the class called Bill Hyman, who, unknown to me, was looked on by his classmates as 'Cock of the Walk' and had a regard for his abilities. The first day I started to play, knowing nothing of his reputation, I tackled him and threw him down, and the next incident was when he made to catch me with the ball, I somehow pushed him off. The other boys were surprised that the rather soft-looking, quiet country boy had the temerity to face up to Bill Hyman and so my reputation as a rugby player was made among my classmates."

His time at school passed happily enough, as he moved through the classes of Mr. Livingston, of Mr. Turnbull (there some specialisation began, for Mr. Turnbull taught only English, history and geography), of Mr. Barclay "a stout, pompous, little man" generally disliked and of Mr. McDougall, the classics master. One incident he records gives a glimpse of the rather shadowy headmaster, Mr. King, who found him sitting one day in disgrace. "I had for some reason been ordered to sit on that form once before and Mr. King saw me there. He came over to me, sat down beside me and in his kindly, nice way asked why I was sitting there." Indirectly too, his memoir, and Allan Yule's, tell something of the school. Both are now old and have been away from school for more than seventy years: both write more legibly still than most boys do. The writing masters must have been thorough in their methods.

The callings of the boys after they had left school give us some idea of the way we contributed to the economy of the land. Of the forty-two boys in his class J. W. S. Wilson remembered the careers of thirty. Three became medical practitioners, among them Charles Duggan who was M.O. with the 19th Lancers in the 1914 war; two were ministers; five, including himself, were lawyers; and four were teachers, including Ben Branford who became Professor at Sheffield University. Two were farmers, one an accountant, one a banker, and one a contractor. One, James Fraser, began in a wine merchant's office but presumably wearied of trade, for he joined the Camerons; another went to sea and there was drowned. Four became commercial travellers, one a jeweller, one a draper and another an insurance agent; one began as a seedsman and changed to hairdressing; another failed to become a veterinary surgeon, took to cab driving and ended as a butcher. It is a diverse assortment of jobs.

The first headmaster was William King, a graduate of Edinburgh, who had been a member of the hospital staff before becoming House Governor of Watson's. In 1870 he had come back to Stewart's, to rule for twelve years, not too successfully: he was a shy man and never robust, a confirmed invalid in the last year of his life. Between his death and the appointment of a successor Mr. W. J. McDonald acted as Headmaster, but was not confirmed in the appointment. Perhaps the slackness in the school under Mr. King made the Governors look outside for a new Headmaster, and look widely. They found a distinguished one, and lost one; for Mr. McDonald developed into a big man, a scholar, a pioneer in geometry teaching, and a power for good in the school. They found instead, under their own hand, William Wallace Dunlop. After six years assistantship in Watson's, and six as Headmaster of James Gillespie's school he was still young but had given clear proofs of his abilities. He accepted the offered headship and guided the school from 1882 to 1911, conceiving his task to be that of administration simply, keeping the machine running smoothly and always master of it, though it grew greatly under him. Till the end of his life, he knew his boys by name and headmark.

SERJEANT PECK.

A cartoon by Tom Curr.

THE COLLEGE

MR. DUNLOP was a great Victorian schoolmaster with the virtues of his kind, above all with the serenity, the sureness of purpose and the confidence given by a life spent in a stable but progressing world. An F.P. who was a boy under him gave this picture, and the affection behind the description adds something to what we learn about the man: "Among the shadows of those fast receding years, still strangely vivid, moves the figure of the old Head, tall, handsome, and commanding, immaculate in frock-coat and shining topper, ruddy of feature with white hair and twinkling with good humour. We see him again in characteristic pose, thumbs caught under the armpits, or with one hand under a coat-tail and the other stroking the smooth white beard, while the colour mounts and glows in his cheeks as he tries in vain to check his mirth at the ridiculous aspect of some hapless youth: and then we hear the ring of his footsteps as he strides down the corridor with buoyant, swinging gait. *Sed haec prius fuere.*"

His first year in school was not smooth. He inherited, and had to end, indiscipline. The same writer said of his beginning, "Stewart's College in 1882 was a small school, badly equipped and ill-disciplined. When classes changed from room to room there was scrumming and confusion almost inconceivable. Few of the old staff had any real control even in the classroom. The way in which Mr. Dunlop tackled the problem was characteristic. He called together the senior boys and asked them if they liked the existing state of things. They assured him that they did not, and he enlisted their sympathy and support."

With their support and help, and some necessary changes in the staff, discipline was restored and maintained. His stature grew with the passage of time and the boys of the nineties recall him now as a distant Jove, paternal indeed but not lacking bolts, and love the memory. Even after his retirement his restless spirit was not still, and he had to find an outlet for his energy in the City Council. His memory for names and faces was proverbial; somehow he kept his hands firmly on a school of eight hundred boys without the help of card indexes. He managed, as well, to undertake all the office work himself, without the help of secretary or typewriter, until a few years before his retirement. Certainly these were years before the bureaucrat grew great among us and demanded his daily ration of paper. Yet even in 1903 George Macdonald, a future Secretary of the Education Department, reporting as H.M.I., to the Governors on the organisation of the four schools, wrote: "I do not for a moment doubt that all the books, lists and statistics that are at present compiled have a use and an interest of their own . . . But are not some of them of the nature of luxuries rather than necessaries?"

The twenty-nine years of Mr. Dunlop's rule changed the school from a struggling infant, of whose survival some members of the Merchant Company were still doubtful, to manhood, and laid down most of the features by which it is recognisable to-day. Numbers increased to a maximum of eight hundred and ninety in 1890, partly as a result of building to the north and west of the Water of Leith, partly through advertisement by the Governors, but largely through the reputation the school gained among parents, a reputation well deserved. From 1870 till 1911 the two Headmasters kept a Register of Distinguished Former Pupils, biassed inevitably in favour of scholastic distinctions, but informative enough. One year will serve as example, 1893-4, chosen because that year Peter Thomsen was first bursar at Edinburgh. (But any other year would do as well—1896, for example, when J. L. Thomson won the Queen's Prize at Bisley.) In the session 1893-4, then, Henry Barker won the Shaw Fellowship in philosophy of £160 a year; W. W. McKechnie added to a Vans Dunlop scholarship of £100 a senior exhibition at Trinity College, Oxford; Peter Thomsen had a bursary of £33 a year; John W. Stewart, John Doig, David Mackie and Alexander Williamson had bursaries of £30 a year. Two other bursaries of £10 a year came from the Town Council and one of £40 a year from the United Presbyterian Church. Mr. Dunlop noted all this carefully, both, probably, because he liked setting down for posterity the triumphs of his boys and because he realised that to parents of limited means the record of success might be an inducement to send us their sons. It is worth saying that these bursaries were paid in golden sovereigns, each with a purchasing power four(?) times as great as our pounds have, and worth while adding that the doors of the universities were open even in the nineties to very poor boys if they were educable.

Organised games became part of school life and the curriculum was extended, sometimes in spite of the Headmaster, who at the end came to hate innovations. By 1907, after many shifts, we began to teach science systematically, in a laboratory designed and ruled over by a qualified science master; in 1912 the first boys sat the Leaving Certificate examination in science. Until 1883 some encouragement had been given by the Science and Art Department (using surplus funds from the Great Exhibition of 1851) which

WILLIAM WALLACE DUNLOP, M.A.
Headmaster, 1882-1911.

had provided equipment, set examinations and rewarded not ungenerously the mathematics master who taught a little science. After 1883 the Headmaster had made other arrangements, engaging a visiting teacher to give weekly lecture-demonstrations. But then, as now, the zeitgeist was clamouring for more and more scientists. In 1900 the Education Department had drawn up a scheme for the teaching of Science in schools, which the Governors declined to follow. Even one of Her Majesty's Inspectors, with a nice sense of relative values, wrote in his report on the school: "A course of Scientific lessons would indirectly benefit the work by the mental diversion and intellectual stimulus which would accrue from such a course." Dunlop himself in 1893, worrying over a drop in numbers, suggested in his report to the Governors that science might be more fully taught, adding prudently, "I think it right to state that except in the case of advanced pupils who can be intrusted to do practical work I do not regard the teaching of science in schools as of much value."

As science grew Greek declined, destroyed largely by the universities which should have fostered it. In 1895 the universities decided that Greek was no longer necessary as an entrance qualification for boys beginning the study of arts, or science or medicine, and, by their decision, deprived it of its central position in schools, till to-day few boys in Stewart's, and none in many schools, study the language, to our great loss.

A necessary addition to the curriculum was art. The present art hall was built in 1909 and Mr. Dick was appointed full-time art master, to replace the old writing and drawing masters who had sought solely to make careful draughtsmen, setting their higher classes to copy such things as "The Stag at Bay", and commending those whose work most closely resembled the original. Mr. Dick and his successors have fostered creative skills and given many wider horizons.

We can judge best the work done in school in the later years of the nineteenth century by looking at the Fifth, the highest form in school, from which boys went off to university and professions. In 1890 they studied four subjects only and covered a good deal of ground in each; that it was done thoroughly we know from the reports of survivors. In English they used as text *Julius Caesar*, the *Knight's Tale*, and four hundred lines of *Piers Plowman*, supplementing this rather lean fare with Nichol's *English Composition*, Mason's *English Grammar*, Stopford Brooke's *English Literature*, Meiklejohn's *History of English Literature* and *History of the English Language*. In Latin they read some Livy, Book IV of Tacitus' *Annals*, *Phormio*, the third book of Horace's *Odes*, the fourth *Georgic* and the tenth book of the *Aeneid*. In Greek they read Plato's *Euthyphro* and part of *Menexenus*, the fourth book of *Thucydides*, Euripides' *Medea*, the twenty-second book of the *Iliad* and some *Demosthenes*. In mathematics they used Euclid I-IV, VI, XI and XII, Todhunter's *Advanced Algebra to Binomial Theorem* and Locke's *Elementary Lectures on Dynamics*, studying as well Geometric Conics and Analytical Geometry. Few Scottish schools of the time did more.

Educationally the school was divided into two sides—Classical and Commercial. There were naturally differences in curriculum between them, but an even greater difference in their attitudes. The Commercial boys were, generally, those who came reluctantly and left early—the IIIrd Commercial was the highest form on that side—having filled in the years between entry and departure as leisurely as was safe. This may be libelling some, but that is the consensus of opinion. In 1886 the school was divided like this:

Form	Age of Boys	Number in Form
V.	15½—16	14
IV	15 —15½	23
III	14 —15	33
IIA ⎱	13 —13½	37
IIB ⎰		36
XI*	13 —14	39
I	12 —13	48
X	12 —13	39
IX ⎱	11 —12	47
VIII ⎰	11 —12	51
VII ⎱	10 —11	50
VI ⎰	10 —11	39
V	9 —10	60
IV	8 — 9	55
III	7 — 8½	49
II	6 — 7	40
I	5 — 6	22
II Commerical 14 —15		42
		(Many dropped out)
I Commercial 13 —14		42

The numbers in some classes seem very large to our eyes, and help to explain why it was possible to pack so many boys into the

* These were boys brought in from outside schools, who had ground to make up, usually in Latin, which we began in Class VI.

building, and to charge fees no higher than £2, 2s. a quarter for the upper forms. In that year there were twenty full-time and six visiting teachers employed, no more: their total salaries did not exceed £3,500.

These were the years when the Scottish Education Department began to exercise its influence over secondary schools, by inspection, by examination, and by the making of grants. The reports of the inspectors make interesting reading now, and give a good deal of information about the work done in the various classes. They are seldom unkind, and when they have to be rude they are politely rude. The first Leaving Certificate examination of the Department was held in 1888, in June, at three different levels—"Honours", where the standard was that of the Indian Civil Service examination; "Higher" where the standard was that of the university preliminary examination in arts; and "Lower", of the standard of the medical preliminary examination. It was an attempt to give a common standard for work in Scottish schools in a limited range of subjects; for the earlier attempts by St. Andrews and Edinburgh University to create uniformity by holding local examinations had failed, the candidates being mainly girls seeking some proof of education. Since 1888 many changes have been made—"Honours" abolished; groups of subjects required after 1908 before a certificate was granted and no longer required after 1950; new subjects—science, art, music, history and geography added; the institution in 1901 and the abolition in 1924 of the Intermediate Certificate as a necessary preliminary to the Leaving Certificate examination, and the like— but this is not the place to recall them. Stewart's sat the first examination with great success. We presented six candidates for "Honours" Certificates, and got eight: so good was the work of two boys presented for "Higher" that they gained Honours Certificates: forty-two for "Higher" and got thirty-nine; one hundred and two for "Lower" and got ninety-one. But I will use no more figures. I had intended to print as an appendix a table of L.C. results since 1888 but have been dissuaded. No figures are used more frequently; no figures are more deceptive. A table of passes would not show that in 1889 many candidates came from primary schools, children of eleven or twelve, and that in some subjects, at least, the standards, must have been very low. Nor do the tables distinguish between those subjects where a handful of selected boys only are presented and those less fortunate in their material. Nor do they distinguish between the teacher and the crammer. Our own figures show too plainly that one of the dullest and least competent teachers we ever had was quite the most successful in getting boys through the examination. Certainly we have never made success in the examination the end we aim at, and have come to it without cramming and without nervous tension. Not for us the rigours of that girls' school of which Sir George Macdonald wrote in 1903: "I altogether demur to the view that two written examinations per week throughout the session are an indispensable part of the necessary preparation for the Leaving Certificate Examination." We can say safely this of ourselves, that few schools in Scotland have had so many passes in proportion to the total number of boys in the senior school.

The other main way in which the Education Department has influenced our lives has been by finding money. The original contribution was small—£250 in 1894. It came to us not directly but through the Burgh Committee on Secondary Education and was conditional on our accepting eight boys nominated to free scholarships by the Committee. The system continued, the amount increasing with the passage of time and the free scholars remaining mostly nearer the bottom than the top of their classes; to be replaced later by a direct grant which we still receive from the department. In that we may count ourselves most fortunate. Without it a very large number of boys would be kept from us, and it is so paid that we are free from the control of anyone except disinterested and very able Civil Servants. Too many of the formerly independent schools have fallen under county council rule.

After 1890 numbers in school began to decline, reaching a nadir of four hundred and fifty-seven in 1914. The Governors were early aware of it and keen to arrest it. For their information the Headmaster in 1893 drew up a report on this decline and the reasons for it, casting quite a little light on the developments of secondary education in Edinburgh incidentally. He drew attention to the opening as a day school, of Heriot's Hospital with fees half those charged at Stewart's. He showed that Gillespie's, the Established Church Normal School and the Free Church Normal School had all added three year courses in higher subjects. The effects at Stewart's were at once obvious: in 1887 seventeen new boys had come from Gillespie's; in 1893 two came. The opening of Craighall School, now Trinity Academy, at Leith, a school offering free secondary education to the university entrance level, also hit us hard. Before 1893 some twenty-five boys came each year from Leith; in 1893 one Leith boy enrolled. Fees at the Royal High School had been lowered. Besides, this was the time when middle-class house building was creating the suburbs to the south of Edinburgh, a district remote from us. There is no doubt that these are the main reasons for the decline in the 1890's; Mr. Dunlop's opinions are confirmed by remarks of Her Majesty's inspectors in their reports. But, later, the decline was accelerated by a slackness in school, the slackness which Mr. Milne had to remedy.

But, even when we allow for that, Mr. Dunlop appears as a great schoolmaster. He turned a struggling little school into one great in numbers and in reputation, he set it on its present path, and left his successor at least the shadow of a great name. We may cast our lilies from full hands.

ISAAC GROSSETT.

" PERKIN "

BUILDINGS

ALTHOUGH numbers increased steadily no substantial alteration was made to the buildings until 1894. Space had been found by bringing into use the western rooms which had been closed in 1870 and by converting the disused chapel into a writing-room in 1883. But that could not cope with numbers which rose from three hundred and twelve in 1881 to eight hundred and ninety in 1890. In 1894, then, the north fore-court was roofed over with glass to give a gymnasium on the east side and a recreation room on the west, so releasing Room 10 which had hitherto served as a gymnasium, and making it possible for many more boys to receive physical education. There had been one hundred and sixty-four in the session 1893-4; there were five hundred and eighty-four in the session 1894-5. The enclosure of the forecourt was disliked by many at the time; they felt that some-thing architecturally pleasing was lost.

The first considerable addition was the art hall, built in 1909 to the plans of G. Washington Browne. It was designed, very successfully, to conform to the architecture of the main building, to which it was linked by opening a door in the west wing. But by 1909 the immediate need for expansion disappeared: members fell steadily, for a variety of reasons, from the 1890 peak of eight hundred and ninety to four hundred and fifty-seven in 1915, and it was possible in 1907 to convert Room 10 into a laboratory, seated for thirty boys without causing violent overcrowding elsewhere. No further additions were made until 1948.

But by 1929 the school was again becoming overcrowded (though the turret room, 23x, had been made into a classroom in 1926) and in some ways old fashioned. Numbers had increased steadily since 1915 from four hundred and fifty-seven to six hundred and seventy-one, and were to increase still further, an increase due both to the great post-war spread of middle class houses in the west side of Edinburgh and to the reputation for scholarship the school was gaining under Dr. Milne. But this does not in itself explain the overcrowding; numbers have not yet reached the 1890 total. Standards of accommodation had improved everywhere and curricula had been increasing in complexity as new subjects, many requiring special rooms, were added. Thus science was now studied by every boy in school; it had already two laboratories and three masters. In the 1890's, indeed until 1907, "Chemistry or

TECHNICAL DEPARTMENT, 1952

[*The Bulletin.*

THE METAL WORK ROOM

Physics up in the turret over the master's room was a joke. The bottles and their contents seemed to have been there since the school was opened". Classical boys spent no more than half an hour a week there, watching demonstrations by a part-time teacher. Educational theory laid increasing emphasis on physical education —Sergeant Grossett in his red tunic, combining the duties of janitor and drill instructor, no longer sufficed—on the need for an assembly hall large enough to house all as a centre of the school's corporate life, on separate geography rooms and the like. There were, besides, private problems raised by overcrowding: the *entresol* above the janitor's room was at once the Cadet store and the place where examination papers were duplicated—a combination useful for recruiting, perhaps; the chapel had to serve as chapel, music room, English classroom, examination hall, etc. During the four continuous weeks of examination in each term the Music and English masters became peripatetic.

Other reasons, too, urged expansion. The new Watson's, soon to be completed, would be " a palace of opportunity"; Stewart's was "destitute of what even the humblest schools in Scotland possess, and have long possessed"—the words are those of the then vice-convener. Other Edinburgh schools were expanding and improving: Heriot's, where the laboratories were already better than Stewart's, was about to build a new Junior School—it was completed in 1934; and the Royal High School Governors were contemplating £37,000 worth of expansion. There was a real danger that the improved conditions in these schools, combined with their lower fees, might deter parents from sending their boys to Stewart's where "the pupils are receiving less than justice and the parents less than they have the right to expect." The full meaning of this remark is brought out in a letter from the Headmaster to the Education Board where he wrote of an infant class of forty. In 1937 the new Headmaster, Mr. Martin, was to re-emphasize it. There were then three hundred and sixty-nine boys in the junior school, divided since 1926 into ten classes, on no logical principle; classes seem to have been added to meet the pressure of numbers at those points where the pressure happened to be greatest. Through these ten classes the boy leap-frogged his way, jumping classes according to his ability. Educationally it was indefensible: the clever boy leaped away from his companions; the near-clever boy who stayed had a grievance; and a core of dull or lazy boys crept its way through the junior school to become a form one or two years older than normal for their stage of development in the senior school. Besides the classes were still too big; the average for the Junior School was between thirty-six and thirty-nine; several were over forty.

To meet this crisis the Education Board had three separate plans for extending accommodation between 1929 and 1948, the first backed by Dr. Milne, the second, which was ended by the war, by Mr. Martin. The third has been realised under Dr. Robbie. Each is worth looking at, for each reflects both the men and the times.

The first plans appeared in 1929, the work of C. E. Tweedie and Sons, after a great deal of preliminary work by J. G. Galloway, the Vice-Convener. They were plans for a building on the site of the present playsheds, restrained and inexpensive in architectural treatment, to cost £23,290. It was to be used to make up for the deficiencies in the school, generally, containing five classrooms and a geography room, three science rooms, two art rooms divided by a movable partition, a craft room and a masters' room. The new building would have satisfied many, but not all, of Dr. Milne's desires. The existing art hall could become an examination hall, Room 6 a library and prefects' room—a curious mixture, and the turret rooms could become stores; but his vision of the present gymnasium fitted with seats and used as an assembly and music room would not be fulfilled.

For the rest of his tenure Dr. Milne struggled along with his overcrowded building, drawing the Board's attention to the need for reform from time to time. After Mr. Martin's appointment a new attack was made. His view was that the fundamental weaknesses of the school were the overcrowding in the Junior school, and the mixing in one building of junior and senior boys. If a reorganised junior school could be housed in a new building the rooms set free in the main building could be adapted to provide the necessary laboratories, library, etc. Clearly the cost was important and there was no doubt that such a building would be cheaper than the composite one of 1929. Within his new junior school Mr. Martin proposed to house thirteen classes, classes 1 to 6 with two sections in each class, and a remove, so offering the boy a systematic progress through the school in classes of reasonable size. A sub-committee of the Finance and Estates Committee was formed in 1938 under the chairmanship of J. G. Galloway and in a very short time, by March, 1939, plans for a new junior school of thirteen (subsequently increased to fourteen) classrooms were prepared. The drawings show a pleasant, simple building, with some traditional features, to be built close to the east side of the main building. Throughout the summer of 1939 the preparatory work went on. By July tenders for the work had been accepted. But there was not time. In October the contracts were suspended by common consent. The only new buildings were air-raid shelters.

In 1942 the Merchant Company had bought Dean Park House, and with it came the considerable piece of land which had been leased to Lord Salvesen, the tenant. The ground offered a possible site for the new buildings, the building offered stone to harmonize with the main building. Accordingly, the Extension Advisory Committee—Mr. Galloway was still a member—considered in 1944 the possibility of building a new junior school on the Dean Park House site, but for various reasons were forced to reject it.

The problem of room became even more acute in 1945. In April a fire destroyed much of the west wing and isolated the turret rooms, forcing us to all sorts of shifts. The coffee room became a steamy, crowded dining-room entered from the playground; classes were held in odd places—in the arctic rifle range, in the prefects' room, in the dining-hall; masters again became peripatetic. Between 1946 and 1950 the possibilities of Dean Park House were reconsidered and sketch plans prepared for a building to give the accommodation of the 1939 scheme. The cost and the difficulty of obtaining building licences forced the Board to adopt simpler means of ending overcrowding. By 1949, when the west wing came into use again, we had some more elbow room, for the ground south of the art room had been used to build two of the post-war, sensible, airy dullnesses of brick huts, to hold four junior classes, dullnesses relieved by Taylor, the gardener, who made the surrounding land lovely with wallflowers and lupins.

The final solution we all know. The instruction in technical subjects, envisaged in 1870, has become real: in September, 1952, Mrs. Wood, the Master's wife, opened a new technical building, made by adding to the south side of part of the playshed. A surprisingly pleasant place has been made with ample light and abundant equipment, divided into three rooms—for woodwork, metalwork and technical drawing, with a smaller storeroom. Already all the boys in the one language course for the Leaving Certificate, and all the G.C.E. boys as well as a few others, have added technical subjects to their curricula.

One of the wych-elms was sacrificed to the new building but the rest remain to screen the north side and harbour the occasional magpie and the jackdaws which nest in the towers. And the elms have acquired better company. To mark the coronation we planted trees in front of the school, on All Fools' Day, 1953. The Master planted a young *John Downie*, the loveliest of the crabs; others planted trees of *Prunus avium plena*, of *malus floribunda*, and of *malus purpurea*. Springs and autumns will be made better by them.

In the autumn of 1953 the new junior schoolrooms were opened.

The architect, W. H. Kininmonth, has very happily made a village group of six separate classrooms, tied to the existing "huts" by a little communal green or quadrangle. The outward walls have been made of dressed Northumberland stone to match the sandstone of the original school, and our education has benefited by watching the masons at work. The roofs have been covered with sheet aluminium which has already lost its first flashiness and acquired a sober patina of grey. Into the rooms daylight and sunshine pour, for the south windows are huge; but the architects have wisely left as many of the original apple trees as they could to make some shade. Inside is opulence of wood—the Master knew about it and had it used well—and of built-in furniture, to make the old building seem like a tenement that has seen better days. And outside, to the south, is great promise—the triangular piece of ground there has been filled with flowering shrubs. Above all the new buildings have made possible the right education of the boys. There is no overcrowding, no leap-frogging, no makeshift arrangements. The junior school now has fourteen classes, two in each of the seven years, of reasonable size and we can hope that the whole school will benefit in years to come from the more careful attention which each little boy can now receive. The cost has been considerable: the technical department and the new junior classrooms have cost more than the contract price for the 1939 scheme.

If the new buildings have given the junior school luxury they have given the main school elbow room; for the four upper classes of the junior school alone remain with us. Science is now housed more adequately: Room 13 is a laboratory and from Room 10 the partition has gone leaving again a spacious laboratory; gymnasts have had Room 3 converted into a junior gymnasium for them; and the tall coffin of a room in the west tower has ceased to be a classroom, its sounding-board no longer collecting discarded trifles, and now houses, temporarily, the library.

For the library is still, after forty years, to be housed worthily. In the number of books it has grown huge, partly by benefactions, mainly by purchase, since a newly appointed Dr. Milne first expressed his discontent at its inadequacies, but it has never been possible to give it room enough, to set aside one place where books can be borrowed or read at leisure. At best it has been a lending library housed in Room 6 and later in Room 13 where boys could scramblingly borrow books during intervals. And yet it is the real heart of the school, especially now when the art of reading is being lost. It may be worth looking back quickly to its origins. The first collection was not a school but a Literary Society Library,

THE NEW CLASSROOMS.

The room on the left was erected in 1948, the other block in 1953.

[*Evening Dispatch.*

formed originally in memory of Thomas White, once president. By 1912 it had grown to three hundred books. The new impulse given to science when Mr. Ross was appointed led, in 1912, to the creation of a science library, never large but holding readable books on popular science. In 1916 the two libraries were joined and housed, as a school library, in Room 6 where Mr. Fortune was librarian. Since then it has grown steadily, swollen occasionally by princely gifts as when D. W. Pentland gave the *Dictionary of National Biography*, to reach two thousand volumes to-day. And we can at last hope that it will be adequately housed. F.P.'s have collected £2,000 to convert one of the existing rooms into a library.

We have been more fortunate with the Chapel, where generations of hospitallers and day-boys have seen something of the beauty of holiness and had their piety quickened by their surroundings. In hospital times the windows were filled with stained glass— protected after a short experience of boys by plateglass—"containing medallions illustrating the leading incidents in the life of Christ with appropriate inscriptions, emblems, etc. The blazon of the founder and his wife (*sic* "Mother" is meant) together with that of the City of Edinburgh and the Merchant Company, the permanent trustees of the charity, are also introduced. Two handsome mural monuments of Caen stone and marble are to be placed here, in memory of the donor and of the late Mr. Longmore of the Exchequer. . . . The floor is to be laid with encaustic tiles, and altogether the chapel promises to be complete and consistent in its character and decorations." The description comes from *The Civil Engineer and Architect's Journal* of 1882.

The Institution of 1870 found no use for it and, with the west wing, it was closed and made forbidden territory until 1883. Then the increase in numbers made it necessary to bring the chapel into use for secular purposes: it became a writing-room, stripped of its stained glass which probably went back to the makers, with long desks facing west, where Williamson taught the handwriting so necessary to an age when the typewriter was a curiosity. Dr. Milne found it so and disliked what he saw, but realised its possibilities. The first improvements were made under his guidance in 1914, as part of the centenary commemoration of Daniel Stewart's death. The walls were panelled to a height of six feet, electric light was fitted and stained glass, the gift of Mr. Fraser Dobie, placed in the upper part of the south window. In the new north window the blazons of Daniel Stewart, of the Macfarlanes and of the Merchant Company were kept. To the walls two brass tablets, one presented by H. K. Rutherford in memory of Dr.

Ogilvie, the other commemorating Colonel R. H. Mackenzie, the founder of the Royal Scots Cadet Battalion, were later affixed, as was the school's pipe banneret. The desks were re-arranged to face north and the place given a rather more ecclesiastical look.

Gifts followed. Michael A. T. Thomson, the Vice-Convener, presented a Trayser bi-manual organ in 1921 and, in the same year, W. F. Russell, returning from Colorado, presented the brazen lectern in memory of his mother. The rest was the work of the War Memorial Committee and the Wallace Dunlop Memorial Committee. By 3rd February 1933 the work was done and the restored chapel dedicated. A desk and chairs had been made for the dais; stalls had been built on either side; oak pews had been substituted for desks; stained glass filled the windows again; and a pipe organ had been built in the choir loft.

The work is described in a speech which Dr. Milne made to the London Club, a speech quoted both for the information it gives about the chapel and for the glimpse of the man who made it. "This great gift of Dr. Hope Fowler's" (the endowment of four Julia Hope Fowler Bursaries of £30 a year in memory of his wife) "enabled the War Memorial Committee and the Wallace Dunlop Memorial Committee to turn their attention to the restoration of the School Chapel. They gave us the stalls on the right and the stalls on the left of the platform, and Mr. John Galloway gave us the handsome electric fittings. It was at a meeting of the War Memorial Committee that someone said 'As for a pipe organ, that is far beyond our means. It would involve not only the cost of the organ itself, but also the large sum required for the reconstruction of the gallery and for the provision of two spiral staircases giving access to the gallery.' Gentlemen, imagine our feelings in that Committee when Mr. Blair said quite quietly, as if he were telling us the time of day, 'I will do that.' He has done it: he has done it to perfection. You will agree that beneficence and munificence of that order paralyse all attempts to express gratitude in any worthy way. Personally, I feel overwhelmed by the kindness of the Vice-Convener to the School.

"My fairy tale is not yet finished. Soon there came the news that Mr. Gilbert Archer, a Master of the Merchant Company and a Vice-Convener Emeritus, desired to present the south window. I invite you to come and see it in the morning sun or at noon or in the winter afternoon's departing glow, as it glitters and glistens in effulgent radiance. Even that was not all: for then there was the east window, which looked so blank and bleak and out of place in its new surroundings: but not for long. You all know Mr. Allan R. Yule who for forty years and more has acted as Clerk of the course at the Annual Sports. That eastern window Mr. Yule has made his own particular concern. We owe it to him. There remained the window to the west and it gave rise to a perfectly spontaneous movement among the present staff and present pupils. No sooner said than done. A few days sufficed for the collection of the necessary money. It was given speedily; it was given heartily; and the window stands as a witness for all time of the love and affection in which pupils and teachers alike hold the place where their days are spent. . . . We needed a guide, philosopher and friend. We found him in the person of a past President of the London Club, who happened most fortunately for the School to be the President of Stewart's College Club. If Principal Smail's gifts to the School are individually intangible, they are not invisible: for it might be said of him, 'if you desire a token of his services, look at the Chapel.'"

The work was completed in 1934 when the ante-chapel was restored to perpetuate in a special way within the building the memory of the dead of the 1914-18 war. Then the stained glass was placed in the windows; the oak panelling to match that of the chapel was added to the walls and entrances; the floor was laid with Craigleith stone and green marble; and the desks for the book of remembrance placed in the corners. On the oak panelling the names of those who died in the 1939-45 war have been carved.*

And so it stands. The architectural purist may criticise the externals but the building has become part of Edinburgh and is acquiring a period charm. It has gathered round itself the affectionate memories of a century of quick generations of boys to whom it has given a pleasant dwelling place with light and sunshine and the hills of Fife to see, with a sense of solid continuity, and with abundant elbow room outside. But inside we are still cramped. The chapel can hold no more than half the senior school; there is still no hall where all the school can assemble, where concerts can be heard, or plays performed. Even classrooms are still inadequate: two masters are peripatetic, with all the inconvenience that results from homelessness. We still need benefactors.

* In the summer of 1954 the Chapel was redecorated with the advice of Mr. Basil Spence. The walls were made white; the roof was painted red and the beams lined with red; the angels on the beam ends were regilded and the organ pipes painted blue.

DR. MILNE'S HEADSHIP

THE new Headmaster, Mr. Milne, reporting on the school in November 1911 had much to criticise. He found a staff that, he alleged, was slack and inefficient: it had become traditional to end the day five or ten minutes before the appointed time; very few had specialist qualifications; some of the heads of departments had reached their position by long service and good conduct only; too many, he told the Governors, taught by hearing lessons which boys had previously learned from a text-book. Even the text-books were doubtful: that for Greek Prose Composition had long been out of print and a brisk trade in old copies went on. For the masters, in fact, it must have been a happy school. Mr. Milne found that, though only two were over fifty-seven, most had been there for quarter of a century at least. Results, so far as public examinations measure them, were deplorable. He could compare the Arbroath High School, which he had recently left, with Stewart's and show that while Arbroath, with a roll of four hundred and fifteen, had forty-three post-intermediate pupils, Stewart's, with a roll of four hundred and ninety-four had twenty-five, of whom eight only were doing post-intermediate work. He could show, too, that many boys were being withdrawn and sent either to other schools or to crammers of one kind or another, to be prepared for the professions.

The school was divided into three groups, on paper—Primary, Intermediate, Post-intermediate, but the attainments within each group varied. The primary group contained twenty-three boys who were qualified to begin secondary work and so earn the Department's grant, while in Form V, the highest form, seventeen boys had still to complete the intermediate work. In other words this intermediate work which in other schools—again he cited Arbroath —was completed by the end of the third year was here spread over five years, to the great detriment of more advanced work. Milne noticed, besides, that the few boys who went further than the intermediate stage had small choice: they might prefer Greek to French or French to Greek: no other choice was open. Science, in spite of the appointment of one science master in 1907 and another in 1908 to meet the requirements of the Department, was not taught beyond the intermediate stage.

Even if we allow for the zeal of a new broom seeing dust

DR. C. H. MILNE.
Headmaster, 1911-35.

where none lay, there was much wrong in 1911. In his long headship, 1911-35, Mr. Milne was to restore the school to its old position.

He was a big man, but complex in character and many found him unsympathetic. He looks at us still from his portrait over the Headmaster's fireplace, and reveals himself in it. The painting is warm with the crimson of a doctor's gown—an F.P. tie incongruously but characteristically accompanies it, but the face above has little warmth. It is reserved, withdrawn, judging the world by its own standards, concealing behind cold eyes the man's thoughts and emotions. We see him too in innumerable, informal pictures, snapshots taken at corps inspections and the like, but there is never a suspicion of informality about him. His gown hangs symmetrical and hieratic, his trencher is square on his head, his face betrays nothing.

All his life he was a scholar. He had graduated at Aberdeen in 1891 with a first in philosophy and came to Stewart's after eight years of classics teaching at Watson's and eleven of headmastering at Arbroath. Yet during these busy years, and the busier ones that were to follow, he gave his leisure to scholarship. His Aberdeen thesis, for the degree of D.Litt., *A Reconstruction of the Old-Latin Text or Texts of the Gospels used by St. Augustine,* was a valuable addition to textual criticism, and after his retirement he was to add an Oxford doctorate to his distinctions. All the ephemeral work expected of a Headmaster was distinguished. Speeches to the London Club, lectures to the Ecclesiological Society, articles in the magazine, letters to the Board, all say something worth hearing in a clear, scholarly way, whether he is defending the teaching of formal grammar, or advocating ceremony in everyday life.

For ceremony attracted him, and he added much to the dignity of school life, even though some of his changes have been done away with. He first insisted on masters being gowned; he began the custom of saluting the cenotaph; he was the main inspirer of the chapel restoration, giving the place he had viewed with disfavour in 1911 its present form. It was a happy chance that the episcopal phase of his long religious quest coincided with the restoration of the chapel, for into the services he was able to bring a little of the beauty of his church, so that to-day, after twenty years, men still remember Cranmer's words which they heard as boys in chapel. To our generation it comes as a surprise to learn that we once sang processionally from chapel to war memorial, took the daily lessons from the school lectionary, or intoned the "Our Father." In the service of the Church and in literature he found the beauty of which so many of his generation, bred in the decaying puritanism of the late 19th century, were starved; in the restoration of the chapel he was a creator of beauty.

His own taste for learning he fostered in school. It is no small thing that four times in seventeen years, in 1920, 1921, 1935 and 1936, we produced first bursars at Edinburgh Universtiy, and that in most other years Stewart's names were high on the list. These were years of fierce competition: the many new secondary schools were increasing the numbers of candidates; there was not then the easy flow of money from Education Authorities to students; to many failure in the bursary competition meant the end of hopes of a university career. The Leaving Certificate results, too, showed a great improvement, even if we allow for the different regulations in force after 1924. From his first coming he saw the need for a school library and managed to leave at least a much more solid collection of books than he found. At his death he left us, too, such of his books as Aberdeen University did not take, as well as £1,500, half to provide an enviable annual income for the classical library, half to maintain the chapel services.

But with all his virtues, he was out of sympathy with many boys and some masters; perhaps he understood them too well but lacked the tact to use his knowledge wisely. He played golf a little but had no interest in games nor in the literature of sport, nor had he any appreciation of the peculiar code of honour which has grown from the playing-field. The interests of Stewart's were first in his mind, and, for Stewart's, the end justified the means. Yet he was conscious of the lack of knowledge and, characteristically, endowed a prize for physical education. The times were against him and we may regret a little his ignorance, for, with knowledge, he might have done something to regulate the cult of organised games in our little world. Certainly he would not have lacked courage; he would not be bullied and much of the odium he incurred was the product of that courage. A library of malicious stories grew round him created, originally, it is to be feared, by at least one incompetent master with whom he was short, and passed to F.P.s Certainly he received less than courtesy from many of the Dunlopian F.P.s, and was often ill-at-ease in their company. Besides he resented and checked some of the pressure which the F.P. Club tried to exert on the school, on the appointment of staff, on the running of athletics and the like.

He had a dry, Dean Ramsayish humour, too dry for schoolboy tastes usually, and a taste for good stories. One that especially delighted him was of the Kirk Officer in a show church who was showing visitors round. "One of them asked if people ever used the church for private devotions, and the reply was: 'Oh aye, whiles. In fact I caught twae o' them at it juist last week.'"

In one important way Dr. Milne, and the school, were fortunate. The day of the old schoolmaster, often ill-equipped, were over. The Scottish Education Department had framed regulations requiring secondary school masters to be honours graduates, trained as teachers in an approved training college; no longer could men hope to rise to senior posts by long service. By 1920 the disappointed old men Dr. Milne met in 1911 were on the way out and his hands were free to pick able young men to fill the vacancies. He picked very skilfully. Almost all his appointments were of men above the average in mental calibre and learning—Mr. E. I. Denoon was among them, Dr. J. W. Oliver and Mr. W. A. Baxter; the present Moderator, the Very Reverend Dr. E. D. Jarvis, for a time taught religion. All gave the school unswerving loyalty and many gave more of their time and energy than could be expected, so that drama, football and cricket, the Corps and the Literary Society flourished, and Europe was opened to many boys. It was a remarkable company of men Dr. Milne gathered round him, their affection for the school making them overlook the Headmaster's shortcomings—and the generosity of the Merchant Company fortified the affection. It was possible, then, to pay masters more than the national scale, and in Stewart's in the thirties assistant masters could hope to rise to £485 a year.

There is a great temptation to write about the staff, a temptation made greater by first-hand knowledge or abundant hearsay; for obvious reasons it is to be avoided. Besides they are not really members of the cast. They are the factotums, scene-shifters, prompters, electricians, producers of the play; but we pay to see the actors. There is one topic, though, not lightly to be passed over. The staff room has been the hub of the school for so many generations of masters, the place where all F.P.s can be sure of welcome and most of recognition. It must be mentioned, for it is *in articulo mortis*.* It is a mean room under the east attic stairs, tall and narrow, with a coal fire on the south side and a window overlooking playground fights and the mysterious comings-and-goings in the bushes and shelters. On the north wall is a book shelf, holding a set and bit of Chambers's Encyclopaedia—the old one—and a history of Freemasonry. The furniture is bent-wood chairs, a long deal form and some collapsible wooden chairs. Contiguity prevents the formation of cliques, all conversation is

* By September 1954 the room was converted into a small classroom. Room 12 has become the new staff-room, adequately furnished and dignified with an Adam fireplace from Balbardie.

general and often, after lunch, resembles a pack in full cry. Any hare does to start the field and there are usually one or two to follow the red-herrings which inevitably appear. Toleration is complete, no rancour follows argument, and there is as much laughter as smoke. It develops one useful quality: any one who has been a member must be able to work whatever Babel he finds himself in. The place is doomed but many ghosts will haunt it, even McGonagall who came once to recite his "Battle of Stirling Bridge."

There is Mr. McIsaac whom a generation nurtured on the Old Testament inevitably called Jake, ginger-headed, and looking in later life rather like a well-disposed walrus. He taught English in the senior school, with astonishing success in Leaving Certificate examinations. "Astonishing" is the word for he was very much a crammer, preferring Stopford Brooke's *Primer of English Literature* to the literature itself. One of his pupils was later to recall that in one year the class read one poem—"*John Gilpin.*" Some of his deficiencies were made up by M. le Harivel who managed not only to teach French and something of French civilisation, but also to introduce boys to English authors and to instil a life-long taste for things French. Of his 1896 class three members—Liddell Geddie, Harry Meikle and Tom Young—were to be decorated with the Legion of Honour for their services to French culture; it would be a matter for boast in a French lycee. There, too, is DOSO, an apt name given jestingly because of his insistence on the spondaic pronunciation of the Greek future of the first person of the verb "to give," "I shall give"; to idle boys the name had a grim connotation. It could serve as his own motto, a proud motto. A small, bearded, bright-eyed man, a scholar and a teacher of infinite patience and pains, George Lyall gave himself wholly to Stewart's. Much of the academic distinction was due to him: he edited the Magazine for a while and it acquired an Attic quality: he took both Rugby and Athletics under his wing, and saw them thrive. With him must come the other scholar of the middle years, W. J. McDonald, a St. Andrews man, later to be external examiner for that university, the author of a pioneer text-book on geometry, who brought not only learning to the teaching of mathematics, but a fatherly kindness which made acceptable his moral lectures. The boys who retain now little of the mathematics he taught remember the moral lectures and his trick of pouncing on their lack of observation.

His namesake, R. G. McDonald is also of the company, a quiet tiger in spite of his growl, given to fits of reverie, the rifleman and maker of riflemen. Whatever else he was, or did, at school is forgotten in that. It is surely the most difficult of arts to teach boys, fresh boys year after year, to become marksmen, to subdue their

OLD MASTERS.

(From a photograph in the possession of Mr. Tom Curr.)

Standing—R. McDONALD. G. LYALL. J. McIsAAC. W. J. McDONALD. C. SYMINGTON.
Sitting—R. T. CURRALL. P. J. MacDUFF. W. H. FARQUHARSON.
On grass—A. A. TOMLINSON.

impatience and discipline themselves to one end. Fate was kind to him and gave him in retirement an adjacent golf course and a neighbour who had shot for India at Bisley. Mr. Strain and Mr. Brough are substantial ghosts. The casual horsedrawn bus which passed the school from the West End needed both or neither if balance was to be retained, so malice said. (We have tended to beef in Stewart's. To another, "Tanky," two boys offered a seat in the football bus.) Tomlinson, talking of swimming, thinking of swimming, being diverted from aorists to swimming by ill-prepared boys, Chalmers with his racy country speech, Dr. Ogilvie disapproving of the row in what was built as his private sitting-room, and a host of others are there listening, perhaps, to D. L. G. on "Agnes in Search of Culture."

One will come as a fleeting visitor, Miss M. E. H. Robertson, L.L.A. (The degree is ended now—Lady Literate in Arts, the devising of St. Andrews University at a time when women were not admitted to the M.A. degree. The university acted as examining body to women who had anywhere followed a course of study equivalent to that for an M.A. degree, rewarding the successful ones with the L.L.A. title and the right to wear a gown with broad blue, diagonal sash.) "Maggie" joined the school as a war-time stopgap and stayed on, the only woman in the senior school, till 1938, none more loved, running tennis, making-up actors—and making their costumes, dashing to Corps camps on a motor-cycle, teaching French with gusto, giving all her energies to Stewart's but remaining a real person. And another, though still in solid flesh, may be allowed into the gallery for the sake of the verse he inspired:

> Beneath your curly pow, John
> Where is there room to stow
> Such learning, wit and kindliness,
> John Oliver, my jo?

The following verse, written by an unkind hand, sets some of the staff before us as a boy saw them.

SCHOOL SONG

> On the highroad to Queensferry
> There dominates a very
> Handsome building, tall, majestic and sedate,
> Where the fussiest of Freaks
> Who is nominated Peaks
> With a dog, a wife and slavey guards the gate.
>
> This is Daniel Stewart's College,
> And an edifice of knowledge,
> And the boys attending there are quite select;
> But the teachers—what a mixture!
> Every one has been a fixture
> Since the memories of our fathers recollect.

E

First there's Jake's abundant figure,
Ever larger, ever bigger ,
Though he races up to school at nine-fifteen
Where he faithfully endeavours
To point out the plains and "revers"
While he ponders where his pucks will be next seen.

That aristocratic joker
Known as Timothy the Poker
Gently slumbers, slumbers gently, on a chair.
On his hand his head is leaning
And his ear he's always cleaning
And depositing the wax upon his hair.

There's the man of Boyle's Laws,
With a sappy pair of tawse,
Who can "caulculate" his answers in a wink.
He has got some funny notions,
But he loves to make explosions
And to mix up fearful compounds for the stink.

There is likewise Mr. Charles,
Who knows all about beer barrels,
And who punctuates his speeches with a "bwoops",
The possessor of a smile
And a chronic fit of bile,
And a face like a tomato when he stoops.

There is Tiger, gentle fellow,
With a voice that's sometimes mellow
And sometimes like the bellow of a bull.
He will nip you hard in places
Which depend upon your braces
If you do not know your syntax or your rule.

There's a gentleman who'll haste not,
With a most capacious waistcoat
And a back that's rather like a motor bus.
To his barrel-like dimensions
Everyone pays rapt attentions,
But old Strainy doesn't seem to mind a cuss.

There is Noble, no one quainter,
Though he thinks himself a painter,
Has an eye that often wanders "doon his bawk".
He will make you pay a penny
For a "pawn o' burnt sienny",
And if you speak he's got "a piece of chalk".

No one dares to ask Old Doso
(He who loves his Latin prose so)
What "just now while I am speaking" clauses mean,
But if a pupil lingers,
Then he wants to "warm his fingers",
And requests him to "return at 3.15".

There's the Man of Mathematics,
Conic sections and quadratics,
Who talks about his tans and sines with force,
He can manufacture posers
All about insulting grocers,
And he thinks that "every quadruped's a horse".

Then next there's Mr. Paully,
Who in the time of holly
Would hang every Christmas tree with blooming tracts.
Do not his feelings jostle,
Though he may be an apostle,
You'll find he is not mentioned in the Acts!

Dr. Milne's successor was Mr. Hugh F. Martin, an F.P., a foundationer by merit from 1894-1901, a classical scholar of Glasgow and Balliol who began his teaching life as assistant to the professor of humanity in Glasgow, and ended it as assistant to the professor of humanity in Edinburgh. He was an infantryman of the 1914-18 war, a company commander of the H.L.I., who delighted in his trade and tried in 1939 to go back to it. As a schoolmaster his career was meteoric. Appointed rector of Madras College in 1920 he stayed there until 1923 when he accepted the headship of Dollar Academy. There his best work was done, rescuing the school from the local education authority and re-establishing it as an independent school with a fair number of boarders. He came to us in 1935 and we might have expected much from his headship, for he had proved himself an able organiser and a man of the large, world, able to rub along easily with all sorts of people, willing to delegate his responsibilities and give himself time to look at essential things. He at once became engrossed in the rebuilding schemes, and his letters show how quickly he saw the important things and went for them. But the times were unkind to him, and made him, who should have been a creator, into a patcher of one wartime expedient after another till the accumulation of worrying detail broke him in health and made him retire prematurely in 1945 after an absence of six months in 1944.

For a year Mr. Frank Ross was acting Headmaster, a man who had grown up with the school in the twentieth century. He had come first in 1907, the first science master in school, and had created the science department *ab ovo*, laying out Room 10 as a laboratory to his own requirements and slowly expanding his department as more boys found the study of science interesting and profitable. Since 1926 he had been deputy Headmaster, succeeding Mr. Lyell. To his short headship he brought great good sense and knowledge of boys, expecting from them a high moral standard and dealing firmly with slackness everywhere. Since 1946 the Headmaster has been Dr. H. J. L. Robbie who has come to Stewart's through Edinburgh and Cambridge Universities, after teaching in Elgin and teaching and rectoring in Bathgate. But he is of the present and must wait for a later chronicler; it is, however, a good omen that the number of boys at the top of the school has substantially increased.

THE WARS

EW things are more difficult for us who were not men in 1914 than to catch and understand the spirit of that autumn of war. Moral indignation, a confidence in our invincibility after a century of little wars, and high patriotism combined to send a flood of eager volunteers to fill the cadres of the new armies. Few of these men brought any military knowledge into the armies; only a very few had served in volunteer units or in Haldane's new Territorial forces and acquired there some skill at arms. What they did bring was something more valuable—soaring confidence and civilian commonsense which ultimately imposed many of its ideas on the military machine. Our own men were little more prepared than the majority. The shooting club and school range certainly had given boys some experience of firearms, but the corps was too young to have had much effect. Their deficiencies were compensated for in other ways. A world, and a school less organised than ours of to-day, allowed them to grow up independent of mind and self-reliant. The city boundaries, too, were more restricted, and most boys could find at no great distance open country for Saturday ploys of their own devising. Whatever the means that made them, these men, civilian volunteers, were to stand, until final victory, against the bravest and most disciplined of all our foes.

The Magazine chronicles their triumphs and, too often, their deaths. Indeed, if we had no other source, we could piece together a pretty fair history of the war—especially of the Royal Scots part in it—from its pages, with one weakness—too few Stewart's boys went to the Navy. The chronicle would begin with the little action of the South African Imperial Light Horse against the rebel Boers —Kemp's commando—where Francis Wightman was killed, and end with the Archangel landing. Each great battle filled the pages with decoration and death notices. The Dardanelles are large here, Loos, the Somme, Soissons, where the 9th Royal Scots suffered so heavily, and the great defeat and victory of 1918. And the smaller campaigns are here too: Dr. Ridley died with the Servian army, one of the little band of Scots doctors who did so much to mitigate the horrors of the retreat; Melville Anderson took part in the destruction of the *Konigsberg* in the Rufigi river. More than eleven hundred former pupils served in the armed forces, of these almost half were commissioned (and some of the best were not).

The Magazine records too, the appalling waste, the loss of a generation of leaders. Some were already clearly marked out for greatness, others had yet to prove themselves to the world but were known at their real value to their friends. There was John Pinkerton, a graduate in classics of Edinburgh, a student at Heidelberg and Berlin, a graduate too of Cambridge, with a first in Semitic languages, who left unfinished his Syriac New Testament, for death found him, a lance-corporal of the Royal Scots. There was John Spenser Jolly, the dux of 1906, assistant librarian of the Royal Scottish Museum, who was killed in action as a sergeant of the Royal Scots. There was Noel Brickman, the most brilliant member of the brilliant fifteen of 1913-14, holder of the inter-scholastic quarter-mile title, who entered Sandhurst in 1914, to die at twenty as a captain of the Cameronians. There was William Beattie Brown, at the beginning of his career as an architect, who was killed as a captain of the Northumberland Fusiliers. There was Grant Gall, a student of music in Edinburgh, Berlin and Paris, recognized in Berlin as peerless in harmony and organ technique, who preferred in 1914 to relinquish a professorship in the United States and serve in the Royal Scots till his death. These are but a few: the list could be greatly prolonged. One more name night be added, for it shows how little time there was, George Cowie's. His Leaving Certificate was presented to his brother; he had died of wounds, a private soldier of the Black Watch, in the August after the examination.

More than two hundred died; how many more is not known, for in spite of all the careful searching, some must be unrecorded. Many had travelled far before coming home for the war, and some must have severed all ties with Edinburgh and with Stewart's. Indeed the list of regiments in which they served is instructive, showing how widely they had fared in the world. The Royal Scots took more Stewart's boys than did any other regiment, with the Royal Field Artillery and the Royal Army Medical Corps—an interesting comment on our supply of boys to the medical schools—second and third, but the Canadian forces are fourth on the list. Apart from the Indian Army and various African forces, where a fair number of Stewart's boys served, the Malay States Volunteer Rifles, the Penang Volunteer Force, the French Army, the ANZAC forces all held former pupils. Other names in the list of regiments sound odd in our ears, names of units raised for service in the 1914-18 war and disbanded at its close, and names of others of older birth which have since disappeared from the army list. Here are the Motor Machine Gun Service and the Highland Cyclists Battalion;

and here too, is the immortal 88th, no longer on the list but deathless in housey-housey schools. One former pupil went to the Connaught Rangers, to win an M.C. there.

We can see other revealing things too in the Magazine photographs, especially the change from the early happy warriors posing proudly in tunics which never knew the cares of the regimental tailor, ill-fitting tunics sometimes of another regiment, with belts askew, to the old soldiers of 1918. They are part of the machine then and have learned to soldier. Collars are boxed up, tunics nipped at the waist, and when the cap is floppy it is art not accident that has removed the stiffening wire.

In school there was a fervent patriotism and spirit of hero-worship, both among the boys and among former pupils. Early in 1914 an F.P. Training Company was formed, parading in the playground every evening in civilian clothing with carbines and belts—too tight often—borrowed from the Corps to be drilled by Tiger McDonald. It lasted till June 1915 steadily losing men to the new armies, increasing its training programme by route marches, by Pentland manoeuvres, even by repelling an attack on the school by Watson's Training Corps. Among the boys hero-worship expressed itself most blatantly when any F.P. returned with a decoration. James Black, coming home with a D.C.M., found himself met outside the Head's room by an assembled school which carried him shoulder-high to the playground through a doorway too low for his head. Mixed with all this was, inevitably, a too facile optimism. To Chalmers and Anderson of the staff in 1914 the Magazine could say: "We wish them all success and hope to welcome them back laden with honours and trophies after their little trip to Berlin." How bitter a trip it was to be the editor learned later at first hand.

Some of the enthusiasm found a useful outlet in manual work. We began in 1916 the system of labour camps which were so valuable in the second war. At Largie first, and later at Banchory, forestry camps were run, extracting a good deal of timber and satisfying the urge for service.

Much thought was given to the best means of commemorating the dead. Already in 1917 a committee had been formed, and subscriptions, invited for a memorial. The money came readily and in 1922, part of it, some £1,700, was spent on the cenotaph which stands in front of the school. It was designed by William Carruthers Laidlaw, an F.P., in form a simple obelisk of dressed freestone, thirty feet high, on a pedestal which is placed on an elevated platform. On three sides are decorative bronze panels with elaborate symbolism recording the names of the dead. The memorial was unveiled by John Buchan (Lord Tweedsmuir) on the 24th February 1922. The rest of the memorial fund was used in different ways: some £500 was spent giving the dependents of the dead help in finishing their education; the sidestalls in the chapel were provided; and some £300 was spent as a share of the creation of the ante-chapel.

The Magazine reflects a different temper in the school in 1939; the moral fervour, the high patriotism, the jingoism, even, of 1914 are lacking. Indeed it is possible to find the university correspondent writing very detachedly, "Among the students there is not much feeling against the war, nor for the war, but, nevertheless, the great majority are quite willing and ready to play their part." The detachment may be undergraduate pose, but 1914 could not have so posed. This is not the place to examine the reasons for the change in temper, which was found everywhere, but it is worth remarking that the nearness of the war to the civilian may have contributed to it. There was no longer the separation between the fighting services—swollen as they were by coiling tails of non-combatants—and people at home; all were equally under the bomber.

The autumn term began late in 1939 and by the time boys came to school air-raid shelters had been made on both sides of the front lawns and plans for evacuation to Nethy Bridge prepared. Indeed the school was forbidden to assemble until adequate shelters were ready. Throughout the first year boys had to add gas-masks in little cardboard boxes to their loads, and air-raid drill was carried out—to the great content of many bored classes, who found a sing-song in the shelters more agreeable than most subjects. From the windows barrage balloons were everywhere visible; Auxiliary Fire Service engines parked in the playground were monotonously serviced and driven noisily round; under the threat of the fire bomb in 1940 fire-watching began—four boys and two masters each night, with Room 13 as dormitory, to use stirrup-pump and sand-shovel on any bombs that might fall; and much time was spent learning how to fight all sorts of fires in all sorts of ways. The fire-watching was not wholly wasted, although no bomb fell, for those who took part learned much of the architecture of the building and more about one another. Some senior boys did more, joining the Local Defence Volunteers, the armleted precursors of the Home Guard.

All these helped to make the war real and near to these in school, as did the souvenir scraps of shell or bomb casing from the raid on Rosyth or the near miss on Inverleith. But nothing did so much as the shift system, the arrangement by which the Queen Street School—not yet named the "Mary Erskine"—shared the building, so that we became alternately morning and afternoon half-timers in our own house. And the west lawn was brought under the plough to grow vegetables, Kerr's Pinks, Victory Swedes, carrots and the like—the onions failed—with thirty boys to plant and tend them. The master in charge earned a brief fame in verse, junior verse:

> " The garden's planted row by row,
> With all the things Gunn hopes to grow."

There were forestry camps, again, at Blackcraig and Hollow Dub, and a long run of harvest camps. Voluntary classes in Russian began after the German attack in Russia had ended the Russo-German alliance and we had found ourselves with a strange ally. The Corps flourished, becoming a J.T.C. and losing the kilt; and after 1941 boys could serve in the A.T.C. There was not at first a separate school flight, but a flight of the 35th(F) City of Edinburgh Squadron had twenty or thirty Stewart's boys. After 1942 "C" flight became a Stewart's flight under our own officers. In short there were many ways in which boys could give very useful service to the country, and be aware that they were playing a direct part in the war.

Again the magazine, recording the lives of the F.P.s, mirrored the war. Here, very early, is R. Galloway, shot down over the Bight, a foundation member of the Stewart's Gefangeners Club. In 1940 J. W. E. Johnson in Stockholm availed himself of the Government's permission to serve with the Finns against the Russian invaders. Dunkirk is here, and the 51st's tragedy at St. Valery, where David Read was taken prisoner. The Russian war made Murmansk a common word. Captain Leslie Saunders, R.N. was awarded a D.S.C. "for distinguished services in taking convoys to and from Murmansk" and Captain Barnetson got an O.B.E. for his work on the same convoys. The citations read baldly at the time: *The Cruel Sea* has since made the meaning plain. The 1st Army's landing in North Africa took T. D. Adie to Tunis, and further. There are gossipy, high-spirited letters from the 8th and 14th Armies, from India and East Africa, recording the lighter sides of war. There are, too, the sadder notices, fewer this time, of death, none more moving than that which records the deaths of the Prydes, where, from one family, three brothers were killed in the R.A.F. "G.A.M." was the first Stewart's boy I knew—we were together in an O.T.C., and no school could hope to be more worthily represented than Stewart's was by him. It was a moving thing when his father pronounced the Benediction at the dedication of the war memorial.

So far as is known eighty F.P.s died. Their memory is still too clear for any words to be necessary. It is not surprising that the majority of those killed were serving as aircrew in the R.A.F. From the R.A.F. came our only V.C., J. A. Cruickshank. His photograph looks down from the first floor corridor wall at passers-by; to the older boys his work is known; but it may be worth quoting the language of the official citation, which tells a great story greatly, for another generation. For his was the best kind of V.C., not the reward for a momentary flash of heroism only, the reward also for the long-enduring self-denial and resolution which self-discipline alone can give.

"This officer was the captain and pilot of the Catalina flying-boat which was recently engaged on an anti-submarine patrol over northern waters. When a U-boat was sighted on the surface, Flying Officer Cruickshank at once turned to the attack. In the face of fierce anti-aircraft fire he manoeuvred into position and ran in to release his depth charges. Unfortunately they failed to drop.

"Flying Officer Cruickshank knew that the failure of this attack had deprived him of the advantage of surprise, and that his aircraft offered a good target to the enemy's determined and now heartened gunners.

"Without hesitation, he climbed and turned to come in again. The Catalina was met by intense and accurate fire and was repeatedly hit. The navigator-bomb aimer was killed. The second pilot and two other members of the crew were injured. Flying Officer Cruickshank was struck in seventy-two places, receiving two serious wounds in the lungs and ten penetrating wounds in the lower limbs. His aircraft was badly damaged and filled with the fumes of exploding shells. But he did not falter. He pressed home his attack and released the depth charges himself, straddling the submarine perfectly. The U-boat was sunk.

"He then collapsed and the second pilot took over the controls. He recovered shortly afterwards and, though bleeding profusely, insisted on resuming command and retaining it until he was satisfied that the damaged aircraft was under control, that a course had been set for base, and that all the necessary signals had been sent. Only then would he consent to receive medical aid and have his wounds attended to. He refused morphia in case it might prevent him from carrying on.

"During the next five-and-a-half hours of the return flight he several times lapsed into unconsciousness owing to loss of blood. When he came to, his first thought on each occasion was for the safety of his aircraft and crew. The damaged aircraft eventually reached base, but it was clear that an immediate landing would be a hazardous task for the wounded and less experienced second pilot. Although able to breathe only with the greatest difficulty, Flying Officer Cruickshank insisted on being carried forward and propped up in the second pilot's seat. For a full hour, in spite of his agony and ever-increasing weakness, he gave orders as necessary, refusing to allow the aircraft to be brought down until the conditions of light and sea made this possible without undue risk. With his assistance the aircraft was safely landed on the water. He then directed the taxying and beaching of the aircraft so that it could easily be salvaged. When the medical official went on board, Flying Officer Cruickshank collapsed, and he had to be given a blood transfusion before he could be removed to hospital.

"By pressing home the second attack in his gravely wounded condition and continuing his exertions on the return journey with his strength failing all the time, he seriously prejudiced his chance of survival even if the aircraft safely reached its base. Throughout, he set an example of determination, fortitude and devotion to duty, in keeping with the highest traditions of the service."

The fitting commemoration of the dead was decided in 1947. To the roll of honour which Dr. Milne had compiled for the earlier war, were added the names and biographies of the recent dead. Mr. W. F. Ritchie compiled the biographies; Tom Curr saw to the scribing, which Miss Norah Paterson carried out; panels, carved with their names, were placed on the south wall of the ante-chapel; a plaque was added to the cenotaph to say that it commemorated also the dead of the 1939-45 war; and money was made available to help the dependents of the dead who might be in need. By Armistice Day 1948 the carving was done, and Tom Curr, as president of the Stewart's College Club, unveiled the plaque and the panels. The service that day was taken by the Rev. D. H. C. Read; on the following Sunday Dr. Taylor of St. George's held another service for former pupils.

But all this is not in itself commemoration. We will understand and remember only if we read carefully and think about the biographies as the pages are turned in the ante-chapel. They are the lively records of our fellows, and they can inspire the meanest of us. "For they gave their lives for the common weal, and in so doing won for themselves the praise which grows not old and the most distinguished of all sepulchres—not that in which they lie buried, but that in which their glory survives in everlasting remembrance, celebrated on every occasion which gives rise to word of eulogy or deed of emulation."

EVERYDAY THINGS I

HIS developing community, like most, needed some means of self-expression. Early ventures had been short lived, mimeographed sheets like the *Harmonic Pencil* that A. L. Curr edited and others of which even the titles are forgotten. These are recurrent ephemerals. III C's *Bizz-Whang Chronicle*— a top-secret document—is the latest. But in December 1910 the first number of the *Stewart's College Magazine* appeared at a cost of threepence, rather solemnly, like most newborn children, to continue steadily till the present day, increasing in price as it advanced in years. Mr. James Walker* was the first editor and to him and his successors we owe much, both for the immediate pleasure of each issue and for the greater pleasure of looking back to old copies and finding the life of the school caught in a series of snapshots, something of the attraction of the well-kept family album. The Magazines record the great and solemn days and events—the battle casualties and chapel-openings, the bursary competition successes and the fires, the Rugby victories and founder's days; they record the careers of F.P.s and find room for reminiscent articles; and they house the first writings of boys and mirror changing literary tastes as they do so. Above all they are our best chronicles of the little things—of playground games, of changes in dress, of hobbies, of the beginnings (and endings) of societies, of Legget's Lot, of French tours, of barrel organs and of crossword puzzles. A random sampling of the lucky dip will help to show the life of the last forty years.

The prefects are there from their beginning in 1917. They were presented with badges of office first in 1919, and their dress shows how little uniformity there was in school uniform then: their ties and badges are all they have in common. In 1935 the senior prefect was dignified as "School Captain" and in 1941 they took over, from the Headmistress of the Edinburgh Ladies' College, the eastern gatehouse, where illegally acquired milk bottles could nestle amid wrecked furniture and the echoes of the forgotten song:

> "Insignes iuvenes
> Viri delecti
> Omnipotentes
> Sumus praefecti"

Who sing it now, to what tune?

* He was later Master of Method for Geography at Jordanhill Training College.

Many boys have received as prefects their first taste of responsible authority; almost all have risen to the responsibility, some greatly, like Harry Robertson in recent years. Their leadership determines the temper of the school, and their success in giving some approach to self-government makes it desirable that they should do more.

The magazine prints, too, the school song, the work of the Rev. G. K. Jenkins and Dr. W. B. Moonie, which has survived in suspended animation, to be revived once or twice a year. The words are not quite as they were first written. To the three houses —Belford, Dean and Ravelston—of 1910 Drumsheugh was added in 1927 and the words of the chorus had to be altered. The cheers which ended it have been happily forgotten.

Wireless came in 1923 when an enthusiast of IIA rigged up a a receiving set in one of the towers. It entered innocently as a hobby; it became a pedagogic weapon after 1939 when D. W. Pentland gave us a central receiver and extension loudspeakers.* But in its first appearance it was merely part of that awakening of scientific interest which began after Mr. Ross became science master in 1907. The field club, after 1912, was one manifestation of it, with papers read on the weasel, and the eel, with trips to Balerno paper mills, to Herdman's flour mill and to a coal mine. A lively vigorous society it seemed, but the 1914 war killed it. Another "scientific" interest was the museum. It began respectably with a collection of butterflies given by Dr. Ritchie of the Royal Scottish Museum, but round it grew a collection, housed in a mahogany case in Room 6, that witnessed more to the acquisitive than to the scientific spirit. Here were juxtaposed some bones of a long-dead Viking, and a Kaffir spoon, a German paper sandbag and a stoat shot by Sergeant Peck, coral from Mombasa and an owl's pellet. It is scattered now, though it survived into the thirties.

Another memorial to the collecting zeal has been the stamp collection. An appeal to F.P.s for foreign stamps in 1929 brought in two thousand. Since then the flow has continued, being diverted to the many boy collectors or canalized into the school collection. The stamp collectors are likely to be with us always. Other enthusiasms have died: the cycling club died in the 1914 war and the sketching club of 1913, though it was resurrected in 1919, lost its vigour and died soon after. Artificial respiration has re-animated the 1928 cross-country club: in 1953 boys who disliked Rugby found themselves conscripted into it and weekly follow a course from Inverleith by Crewe Toll and Fettes.

One child of the twenties has confounded the prophets: in 1925

---

* It was replaced by the Board in 1947 by a more up-to-date set.

the crossword had so established itself that a boy could offer Mr. Denoon a Latin version, but the writer of that note was sure the fashion was fleeting. Yet by 1931 the staffroom knew *The Listener* —and still knows it—and an F.P., J. Liddell Geddie, the editor of Chambers's Dictionary, became a public benefactor. With the crossword, as the photographs show, came lengthening plus-fours as dress for golf and school, and a friend, long absent, the barrel-organ in the back road churning out "Show me the way to go home". There came, too, a nasty import, the charleston, rearing its ugly heels in cloakrooms. Buses increased in number. No longer had the editor to say, as in 1915, that the bus from Blackhall to the West End would resume service on September, 30th. Now an elite developed, of "upper deckers," on frequent buses. Biscuits were then three a penny and touch-rugby, played with a short stick for ball to rules based remotely on those of the Union game, caught on. It can never have been popular with parents; clothes suffered. The Victorian bandalore made its silly reappearance in the thirties to go underground and reappear in 1954.

But these were passing crazes. More firmly rooted have been conkers and bools, cocky-rosie and cuddy-wechts. The last is temporarily in eclipse—clothes rationing may have caused it to be frowned on—but cocky-rosie still returns to the junior school with the swallow and raises its little song to say that summer has come back again "Last up's het at cocky-rosie." The other summer festivals of the early years of the century—the display of gymnastics and morris dancing on the west lawn and the tennis club party— tennis and croquet in the afternoon, dancing at night—these are gone and we are poorer for their going. Gone, too, is the little fourteen-hole golf course which lay once to the west of the tennis courts.

School uniform kept on changing. The colours had begun as blue and red—broad blue and narrow red in the mufflers of the nineties. In 1895 the cap became black with a version of the Stewart arms embroidered in front, and the colours changed to red, black and yellow, to delight a Roumanian visitor of 1895 who was "very happy to meet a Roumanian-speaking English boy and see my country's colours at the necks of the little Scotch boys." (The Roumanian-speaking prodigy was known, too, for his gadgets, for cowbell tiepins that tinkled disturbingly when gently touched by a pen and flowers that squirted water. . . .) The shades of red and yellow were changed in 1916 but until 1924 boys wore, apart from uniform ties and stockings, whatever clothes they fancied. On 1st October of that year the Vice-Convener, Mr. Fairbairn, presented each boy with a new cap of his own designing, very much like the present one except for the badge which was embroidered in red and gold. The Magazine preserves a facsimile of the copper-plate letter of thanks, signed in a boyish hand, now that of one of Her Majesty's Inspectors. With the cap went a black blazer with embroidered badge and red and yellow piping. The new badge in heraldic colours came in 1930, and in 1938 regimentation followed; the Magazine noticed that blazers and school stockings must now be worn and regretfully added, "Fawn jackets over pea-green trousers are now taboo." Since then there have been two changes: a subversive movement among the boys to replace the black by red stockings has succeeded, though authority has diminished the victory by altering slightly the shade of red to a less revolutionary one and defining authoritatively the shades of both red and gold; and in 1953 the badges on the blazer of first XV and first XI boys were altered. The splurge of letters and dates, like long-service medals or the festal dress of an American confraternity, has been replaced by a crested badge with the Roman XV or XI below it. These badges were the gift of one of our Vice-Conveners, J. C. Smith, who made the 1924 caps.

In the twenties foreign tours, in which we were pioneers, began. In 1923 M. Meslier and Mr. Hardie took a party of boys to Amiens and Paris. That was the beginning of a succession of visits, taken over after a while by Mr. Grant, usually during the Easter vacation, to France, or Belgium, or, more recently to Switzerland. The *Neuralia* schoolboy trips to Scandinavia were used after 1931, but these were not specifically Stewart's. Nor were the cadet tours of the battlefields; they were made by Stewart's boys as members of a larger Cadet force. More interesting and more valuable, perhaps, has been the practice of attaching parties of the present Combined Cadet Force to battalions of the Rhine Army for training during the Easter vacation. The first party went in 1950 to Minden with the Rifle Brigade. All seem to have learned something of Germany, as well as something of modern weapons and infantry training.

The Magazine records, too, the comings and goings of our guests. We have twice had strangers in residence. The first war brought us from Flora Stevenson School four classes, driven from their own place by military occupation, housed partly in the Art Hall, partly in school, to cause Dr. Milne some care. "Some measure of anxiety as to the effect is inevitable" he wrote in 1916—a private letter. But what his anxieties were, or whether they were justified he never said; probably he feared brawling. The Flora Stevenson classes stayed with us till 1919. Hitler's war brought from Edinburgh Ladies' College girls to alternate morning and afternoon with us. Their stay was shorter, but they presented us with a French dictionary—still in use—at their going.

These are all little things. And if the Magazine gave no more than little things it would be still worth skimming through. But it does more. It gives a full account, year by year, of the activities of the bigger things, such as the Corps.

Even before the Magazine began the school had felt the wind of rearming. Lord Roberts was pressing for conscription; Haldane, the Secretary for War, was calling into being the Territorial Army and Officer Training Corps; already in 1909 Dr. Darling noted in the Visitors' Book the need for a school Corps. But we were late in starting—perhaps the reluctance to innovate which settled on Mr. Dunlop as he grew older had something to do with it—and as a result, Stewart's was forced to content itself with forming part of the Cadet force, while Watson's and Heriot's had O.T.C.s.

At a meeting in March 1913 Colonel Mackenzie, the C.O. of the Royal Scots Cadet Battalion spoke to the boys about the Cadet force. Volunteers came forward and on 11th March 1913 Stewart's cadets were embodied as C. Coy of the 1st (Highland) Cadet Battalion, The Royal Scots Regiment. They carried the carbine in place of the rifle and wore a uniform that 1914 was to drive out of the army—well-fitting scarlet doublets, hunting Stewart kilts, white belts and spats, red and white hose tops and a serviceable leather sporran, useful for haversack rations. The first public appearance was 20th May 1913 when a detachment formed part of the guard of honour for the Lord High Commissioner to the General Assembly. The armoury in the west gatehouse was fitted up in 1914; a rifle range was already available—in June 1902 Sir Archibald Hunter had opened the new safety rifle range along the Ravelston Terrace wall, to be replaced in 1937 by the present range. Recruits came in steadily; by the end of the war the company, under Mr. F. Ross, was eighty-four strong, boys over the age of fifteen being encouraged to stay on by knowing that their service above that age counted for the Territorial Efficiency Medal. Their parade-ground bearing seems to have been valued; in 1914 sixty of them formed part of a royal guard of honour, one hundred strong, at Holyrood; they were repeatedly called on to furnish guards for the High Commissioner and once for the Crown Prince of Japan. These were memorable parades to those who took part in them. Another was to become legendary, when the inspecting officer at an annual inspection, stepping to the edge of the terrace to address a parade drawn up on the tennis court, somersaulted down the slope "buits and spurs and a." At some time the battalion was presented with a King's colour and this, when the Stewart's corps became independent in 1923, remained in our possession.

From 1923 till 1935 the Cadet company remained autonomous,

losing the government grant of 5/- a head. In 1935 the War Office sanctioned the change long desired and the company became an O.T.C. enjoying all the advantages in equipment, finance and training of the higher status. The change had one drawback: the scarlet doublet was replaced by khaki, which had been working dress since 1918, and the last Edinburgh example of the dress of the old Line was gone except for the drummers who have managed to retain scarlet in spite of the battledress that came in 1940 with the change from O.T.C. to J.T.C. and later to C.C.F.

The present state of the C.C.F. is best summarised in two sentences of Lt.-General Sir Colin M. Barber, G.O.C.-in-C. Scottish Command, written as part of his report on the Corps in 1952. "This unit is playing its part in preparing future leaders. The training is good and the contingent is extremely well admininstered."

Reference has already been made to the £2,000 raised by the F.P. club for our library. The school has attracted other gifts— from the stranger without the gate, from vice-conveners, from F.P.'s, from parents. Of these a full list is published annually in the *Report of the Company of Merchants*. Sir Dhunjubhoi Bomanji, greatly impressed by the bearing of our boys, gave £400, now used for prizes in mathematics and athletics. The Hugh F. Martin prize in Art (established by Mr. George Dobson) and the Kennedy Fund for the C.C.F. Band are examples of the interested generosity of Vice-Conveners. From F.P.'s we have had such gifts as Dr. Hope Fowler's munificent endowment of University bursaries, the £500 with which Mr. John G. Galloway backed his advocacy of a new Junior School, the £250 received from the trustees of A. J. Lethem as well as such funds as provide the C. W. G. Taylor prize, appropriately enough for elocution, the Eadie Davidson, Hutton, and Gardner Thomson prizes (all established in memory of brothers). To the grief of sorrowing parents we owe such prizes as the Norman Waddie and Norman Gardiner prizes and to the gratitude of old foundationers such bequests as the Proctor and Rutherford prizes. £250 for the maintenance of the sons of ministers' widows and the £1,000 already referred to "that some other poor kid might profit." "*Gratis accepistis, gratis date.*"

If there were time and space one could use the Magazine as more than a hoard of facts, and try to find in its pages the changes in outlook and taste of the past forty years; for presumably each editor has published those things which his public expected to find in the Magazine. That is too big a task for this chapter: we really need an anthology of our own prose and verse from the Magazine. But even a cursory reading shows the changes in style and the strong journalistic sense of our younger writers. Few headlines escape

them and there is often a happy turn of phrase. Flying saucers
and their occupants,

> "Do they come from Venus?
> Or do they come from Mars?
> They come in things like rubber heels
> And some are like cigars."

the taking of the stone from Westminster,

> "O Saxum regale ceperunt
> Et a templo traxerunt,
> Cum angli Saturnalibus
> Ebrii et beatissimi fuerunt,"

Kon Tiki (in Murray's metre),

> "He cut a log of balsa from a muckle balsa tree
> He hackit it and choppit it and sailed it on the sea."

and a host of other topics provoke verse or worse.

One year will show the change in style. In 1929 the Headmaster
—a Victorian—wrote, "I value greatly your personal intercourse
with the boys because of the elevating effect which it has upon the
general tone, more especially when it is combined with that of
Shakespearian dramatic art." In the same year the school notes
could say of the editor : "A fresh guy will sure be handed the frozen
mitt" and of the new Vice-Convener: "he presented his credentials,
which were OK'd." These are extremes. There are more subtle
and interesting changes.

F

EVERYDAY THINGS II

FOR long the school lived in armorial crime, probably through an omission of the founder. Daniel Stewart assumed an armorial coat, but failed to matriculate it. The arms were those carved over the door of the main entrance showing in the first and fourth quarters the rampant lions of Scotland over the chequered fess of the Stewarts and in the second and third the garbs, or sheaves, of the Cummings, Earls of Buchan. They are proud arms, but for long the school used, and blazoned on the organ-gallery, prouder: the first and fourth showed simply the lion rampant in a tressure of Scotland, the second and third the garbs of Buchan, the arms, in fact, of that Earl of Buchan who fell at Verneuil in 1424, fighting for a resurgent France against England.

The original arms, which were matriculated in 1917, are, reputedly, based on those of Sir Alexander Stewart, son of the Wolf of Badenoch; reputedly, for though Sir David Lindsay's Armorial of 1542 shows the arms of the Wolf's descendants as carrying the fess in the first and fourth, the arms on the seal of Euphemia Ross, the Wolf's widow, are very different. Whatever their origin, however, the fess and the garbs were the ground of the arms of many who claimed descent from the Wolf's son, of Stewart of Balnakeilly, of Stewart of Ladywell, of Stewart of Garth.

Presumably Daniel Stewart was led by the frequency of such arms among the Perthshire Stewarts to take similar, surrounding them with a bordure charged with mullets as a mark of difference, and adding as motto words not inappropriate to one of the Wolf's litter "Never Unprepared," a motto which Stewart of Balnakeilly uses in the Latin form "*Nunquam non paratus.*" But the question remains. What reasons had Daniel Stewart, the son of an Appin crofter, for thinking he was sprung of this branch of the house of Stewart?

The blazon over the inner entrance was the gift of Sir Will Y. Darling. After praising the motto in a Brains Trust broadcast in 1944 Sir Will found that it was nowhere displayed in the entrance hall at school. His gift was, in part, an attempt by one who, self-confessedly, came never prepared to school, to inculcate the virtue of preparedness in others.

From the inner porch the transition to janitors is an easy one, for there they have their station. Since 1870 they have contrived to turn themselves into institutions, uniform in the dignity of tail-coat and top-hat, but each strikingly individual, and each a power in the place. None since Isaac Grosset, 1873 to 1912, has acquired his autocratic status, but each has done much to bring some law into the jungle of breaks, ruling by no inherent right but by force of personality. William Anderson, Bob Guthrie and now Alec make up the succession, with a great diversity of experience behind them, so that while one generation of boys learned, in talk, of the rigours of redcoated soldiering for the Queen, another now learns of frozen seas, of penguins and of whales. At Inverleith, too, the groundsmen, from Peter Bell who came to a rough pasture in 1895, have made themselves part of our world, more fortunate than most; for, while generations of boys pass quickly and our work with them, the turf, which is their real delight, grows greener and smoother as the years pass, in spite of the damage done by trespassing foot-ballers. There is no need here to say anything of Jack Wright. He has been coach, counsellor, universal aunt, and friend to two generations now, the essence of all that is Inverleith.

For half a century and more the Literary Society has flourished, an expression of the histrionic and rhetorical talent of the school. And it had predecessors. The Third Classical Literary Society of 1886 had a vigorous leader in William Archibald Thomson; doubt-less there were others unrecorded. But the Society as it exists to-day came into being in 1897 with William Cowper Robertson, "Poet" Robertson, later to be minister of the Scots Kirk in Paris, as its president and Charles Cummings as secretary, a society of both present and former pupils at first until a disapproving Master in 1913 had membership restricted to pupils. It met in school, at first on Saturday afternoons and later on Friday evenings, to hear papers read, to debate, to hold annual picnics with guests invited, to organise an annual concert in chapel, and to produce plays, or scenes from plays, such as *Midsummer Night's Dream* with girls co-opted to play female parts and a future historiographer royal as Theseus. It attracted to itself, and still attracts, the best of the school. Perhaps the truth of this is best seen in the session 1902-3 when the president was John Pinkerton, the future Semitic scholar, the vice-President was Thomas White who accomplished much in the I.C.S. before his untimely death— *A Good Day's Work* records his life—and the secretary was James Munro, later to be lecturer in colonial history in Oxford and Edinburgh.

The war years were blank. The society, like so many others, died and was not revived again till 1919, so that it was not till 1952 that the first and second presidents could return to celebrate the jubilee. But it came to greater life after the five years' death, especially, with Dr. Oliver's inspiration, in the acting of plays. The hesitant first steps of 1924, when scenes from *Henry IV, As You Like It, The Merchant of Venice* and *Julius Caesar* were produced in the gymnasium, soon became confident and year after year the society produced a Shakespearian play—*Julius Caesar* in 1927, *Twelfth Night, Macbeth, Midsummer Night's Dream, As You Like It* with *She Stoops to Conquer* and *The Rivals* interlaced, plays which gave a taste of acting to a large number of boys and enabled some to develop into very competent actors; Cyril Jones' Lady Macbeth was memorable, and so was David Read's Kate Hardcastle; Tom Fleming is one of the most successful of present-day radio actors.

The 1939 war stopped dramatics—a glass-roofed gymnasium has drawbacks—and there had again to be a fumbling revival while acting ability was nursed. We began with one-act plays—*The Changeling, Alfred and the Neatherd* and the like juvenilia. But by 1950 the society was confident enough of its powers to stage *Murder in the Cathedral* with the chapel as theatre, to stage the best of its productions, and, more ambitiously, to offer *The Lady's Not for Burning* in the Cygnet Theatre and *Androcles and the Lion* in the Laurieston Hall, the first in 1951, the second in 1953. Perhaps it was part of the charm of *Murder in the Cathedral* that it was a domestic production, the last in which we entertained parents and friends at home. It is most unfortunate that we should have to do these things in the hired houses of strangers.

The minute books show the other activities of the Literary Society. There are inaugural lectures by F.P.s or visitors—Arthur Matheson on the " Scots Advocate," W. F. Arbuckle on the " Scottish Castle " or Principal Smail on " Beauty and Utility "; there are papers on a variety of topics by members—one night "Witchcraft," "Films," "Beekeeping," "The Betrayal of Warsaw" and "Perthshire" were all offered; there are endless debates on debateable topics—"That the Discovery of America is to be Regretted"; "That we should judge a composer by the standard he sets"; "That the Victorians are our betters"; there are debates with other schools, two or four-side, best attended when the ally or opponent is a girls' school; there are play-readings, *The Playboy of the Western World, The Rehearsal* and the like; there are Record nights and Masters' nights; and there were Balloon nights when chronology was ignored and like men of various ages—Ralegh, Edison, Newton and Cavendish—were set free to talk. More recently the wireless has given new forms of linguistic exercise, "Brains Trust" and "Twenty Questions."

Through all the minutes there runs a low refrain, "It is regretted that the Opposition backbenchers had on occasions to be called to order" or "Certain members then raised objections to the rowdiness of the meeting." It is the price paid for admitting too many immature boys with a taste for a Friday evening's outing and some skill in playing the fool. But for the majority the society has done great good in encouraging them to speak with confidence in public—the defect of our Scottish education is that our boys are too often literate but inarticulate—to submit their words to the rough criticism of their equals; and it has given many new tastes in cultural things. In another sense, too, it benefits its members: alone of school societies it has remained autonomous, free of all but the mildest magisterial scrutiny, a schoolboy society the officers of which must run it themselves.

Musically we have been as backward as the majority of Scottish day schools, treating what is essential as subsidiary, making music, which should be fundamental, one of the lighter options, or diversions of the curriculum. Not till 1945 was music made a compulsory subject for all boys. It was a curious attitude of mind, sired by puritanism out of utilitarianism. But now there is promise of better things. There had been certainly a band of sorts in the Hospital; Dr. W. B. Moonie, a distinguished composer himself, who followed his father as music master, began in 1921 to get together an orchestra, with little encouragement and little success; the re-creation of the chapel made it possible to build a choir and Mr. Blair's gift of the organ did something to enrich our musical life. But it was not till the Mastership of Mr. Iver Salvesen that the orchestra became a musical reality. His encouragement and support have inspired others, and gifts of instruments or of money to buy instruments have fallen on us, so that we have to-day an orchestra complete in strings and with a fair wind section, though deficient still in oboes and bassoons—these are costly—French horns and percussion instruments. Boys are taught to play their instruments by visiting teachers, though the work of keeping the orchestra in being and working as a unit is done by the music master. Of the development of school music since the war no better proof can be had than this, that we have been able, without outside help, to stage three light operas—*Trial by Jury, The Pirates of Penzance* and *H.M.S. Pinafore.* Those of us who heard *Jesu, joy of man's desiring* at the 1954 closing concert need no other proofs. But in all such work there is the weakness which comes from our short generation: no sooner does a boy become competent as an instrumentalist than he must leave. The full value of the orchestra to players and public will not be had until an F.P. orchestra is formed. It would permit our seedlings to become plants, and their active lives as players would be much longer than in other F.P. Clubs.

That mention of an F.P. orchestra must serve, at last, to introduce the subject of F.P.s. There is much to commend the idea of taking as a text "By their fruits shall ye know them"; and of writing the history of a school simply in terms of its former pupils; for no school is an end in itself; each is judged ultimately not by the ephemeral results of schooldays—successes in bursary competitions or Leaving Certificate examinations—but by the kind of men it makes. Perhaps the difficulty of such a history deters us from it; we know so little about so many of our F.P.s. The Magazine here is apt to delude us. It records the successes which are recordable and easily appraised, and, being edited by schoolmasters, it is apt to lay too much stress on university successes. Besides it is so easy to read in the *Scotsman* that X has been awarded the degree of Y by the university of Z and to transfer the information from newspaper to Magazine. It is easy, too, to run through the list of birthday honours and notice the O.B.E.'s and C.M.G.'s bestowed by grateful sovereigns on their servants. It is not at all easy to find out about, or to appraise, the slow promotion in industry or business of the majority of our boys, and yet their work is usually done no less well and is of no less importance. But with these reservations, it is still worth looking for a little at some F.P.'s and trying to find from them what we give to the world.

We appear to specialise in producing the sons of Martha, the workers who get things done and who regard the job more than their status. Many went to the old Indian Civil Service to help perform that miracle of honest government which was undivided India. Thomas White might serve as their type, or Sir Walter Booth-Gravely, who became acting governor of Burma. Others, in the Home Civil Servie, have risen to great office—Sir John Glen, Sir William W. McKechnie or Sir David Milne. The colonial service took many—James Craig to Egypt, Pat Hendry to Zanzibar, J. T. Rousseau to Tobago, Sir Gordon Lethem to Guiana. A few regular soliders have come out of school—Major-General Lyon-Murray, William Stevenson Jaffray, who became commandant of the R.A.Ch.D., and, since 1945, a fair number who have yet to distinguish themselves. Of professors there has been a notable crop, especially at the turn of the century when Scots professors were in demand overseas; William Caldwell, the author of *Pragmatism and Idealism* at McGill, J. Macgregor Smith in Alberta, Andrew Stewart, the present Principal of Alberta, William S. Smail at Grahamstown before going as rector to Perth Academy, his brother, Principal of the Heriot-Watt College, J. Eadie Tod in

Belfast, W. B. Stevenson, the Hebrew scholar, and John Walton, the botanist, at Glasgow, or A. A. Matheson, Professor of Scots Law in Dundee. There are some men of letters—Liddell Geddie, George Malcolm Thomson, and James C. Corson; some musicians such as Frank Collinson and W. B. Moonie; and at least one distinguished artist—Sir W. Russell Flint, whose biography *More than Shadows* deserves to be better known in school. The Church in its greater days took many, including a Moderator in Dr. C. W. G. Taylor of St. George's, some of the most distinguished, like George M. Gibb, the dux of 1883, to work devotedly in remote parishes with no thought of advancement. David Read, J. D. A. Macnicol, James F. Whyte, W. J. McDonald and James Barr—all duxes—entered the Church after graduating with firsts. Medicine took more, none more devoted than Dr. Hope Fowler, a pioneer and victim of radiology; and some have become schoolmasters—John Bowie, the rifleman and curler, G. L. Turnbull and Peter Thomsen. I will not prolong the list. F.P. readers will be able, each from his own contemporaries, to extend the list and see my generalisations exemplified and to complain that, like the Magazine, I have ignored those whose careers were outside the professional world. It has seemed to me best to try to show that we have produced many able business men by noting in the lists of Vice-Conveners and Masters those who were F.P.'s; for these offices imply that their holders have been rated high by their fellow members of the Merchant Company, the best judges. To that list we must add at least the names of Sir William Frazer, the General Manager of the North British and Mercantile Insurance Company, E. F. Spaven, the Secretary of the National Bank, Laurence Kinnear, the Secretary of British Oxygen Ltd., Jackson Wallace, Chairman of Mac Fisheries and G. I. Stewart who is not unknown in the Investment Trust world.

We hang together as few people do. The Magazine suggests that whenever an F.P. finds himself in a strange place he looks round once or twice before settling down, hoping that he will find another F.P. with whom to form a branch of the F.P. Club. The first volume of the Magazine in 1911, records a small but lively British Columbian branch; the second volume a South African branch; in 1952 the F.P.'s in North America were so far organized, and benevolent, as to endow a prize for North American history. The mother hive is the Stewart's College Club (its members distinguished since 1931 by the lion-spangled tie), a vigorous stock, from which many societies have swarmed. The Club was reconstituted in 1901 from the omnibus Stewart's College Athletic Club of 1886 and in 1929 Dr. Hope Fowler presented it with the Presiddent's badge of office. Early in 1905, the most important of the provincial clubs, the London Club, was founded. It times its annual dinner judiciously to coincide with international football matches, and a series of energetic secretaries has kept it vigorous, supporting the school in all sorts of ways, whether by entertaining itinerant boys or by raising money for the library.

The smallest and most exclusive club, and one doomed to extinction in a future that we hope will be very distant, is Legget's Lot. None but those at school between 1898 and 1900 may attend the dinners which R. L. Legget first organised in 1938.

In the early part of this century the club took a much more active part in the running of the school than it does now. The School Encouragement Committee was a very lively body and little that happened at school escaped its notice. The Committee had much to do with the founding of the Magazine and of the Cadet Corps; it was constantly urging the Headmaster to fill vacancies on the staff with men capable of coaching games, and expressing displeasure when he disregarded the advice offered; it pressed him to allocate boys early to their houses; it supported the Literary Society in a dispute with the Headmaster; and it even, on one occasion, talked of raising a subscription for a master who resigned after a quarrel with the Headmaster. One of Dr. Milne's troubles was that he resented this encouragement and resisted it, so alienating many well-meaning F.P.'s.

CLASS TEACHING IN THE 1890's.

Elementary Lower Division.

[From an old Prospectus.

MISS COCHRANE WITH HER ELEMENTARY LOWER DIVISION.

INDIVIDUAL WORK IN CLASS 1B BEFORE THE TRANSFER TO THE NEW CLASSROOMS, 1952.

INVERLEITH I

HE athletic cult which was to develop so enormously in the late nineteenth century Britain affected us early. Already in the seventies F.P.'s had secured the use of the north-east ground floor room—now a laboratory—as a gymnasium after school closed. It was fitted with a horse, bars, rings and other gymnastic gadgets, and there a number of F.P.'s came one or two nights a week—to the annoyance of Grossett—for exercise. Most of them played football for one club or another and the gymnasium work was varied by road work. From these meetings, at once social and athletic, came the Stewart's College Athletic Club. The Club was formally constituted at a meeting in 5, St. Andrew Square, on 4th March 1886. Mr. Dunlop seems to have shared the suspicions of most Headmasters of the time about the value of the cult of the body and at first gave it grudging support. He consented to act as Honorary President and another master, W. J. McDonald, was President, but most of the work, and inspiration, came from Finlay D. Cameron, the secretary, and A. R. Yule, the treasurer. They organised an omnibus club with many parts:—

> Stewart's College (P.P.) Cricket Club,
> Stewart's College (F.P.) Cricket Club,
> Stewart's College (P.P.) Football Club,
> Stewart's College (F.P.) Football Club,
> Stewart's College Tennis Club,
> Stewart's College Cycling Club.
> (The safety bicycle was coming in and organised runs were popular.)

The Club was responsible, with little help from masters, for developing football, cricket and athletics in school. F.P. representations helped to induce the Merchant Company to rent Honeyman's field at Ravelston—windy Ravelston with its hills and dales—as our first playing field proper. It was the piece of land, now built up, between Ravelston Dykes and Queensferry Terrace, leased in 1886 from the governors of the Trinity Hospital for £8 a year. Three adjoining cottages were also rented, one to serve as a pavilion. It was a school field but F.P.'s were allowed to use it after seven o'clock on weekdays and after four o'clock on Saturdays. Our stay there was short. In 1894 the Merchant Company, after inspecting several pieces of ground, bought for us the Inverleith field from the Rochead family. It brought with it an unexpected privilege—the right to three sittings in St. Cuthbert's Church.

At Ravelston on 21st May 1887 the first sports were held, on a day of broken weather, with a full programme including four events open to all and five events confined to F.P.'s It might be worth noticing that at least one "penny-farthing" race was included. The "penny-farthing," or high ordinary, two-mile bicycle race in 1888 was open to members of Stewart's College Cycling Club. It was won by John W. S. Wilson (scratch) with R. W. Hepburn (60 yards) second. Wilson quickly overtook his opponents and won by about fifty yards. Age has not dimmed his enthusiasm; at ninety he still frequents Inverleith.

From then till the present day the sports have been run for the School by the F.P.'s, though latterly masters have taken an increasing share in the work, especially Mr. Hardie who was honorary games secretary for twenty-seven years. Many will remember the share of the late Jock McGregor in the logistics of the sports, and Allan Yule, Clerk of the Course for fifty years, and still to the fore at the age of ninety-five.

Since 1895 the sports meetings have been held at Inverleith and in that larger and flatter arena performances have improved and there have been more opportunities to use the meeting as an annual reunion of F.P.'s, parents, kin of lesser degree, staff and boys, where we can meet, talk, admire offsprings' prowess and disapprove of present arrangements for running the sports, especially the change to the Union field. (This will always be a good subject.) The weather is nearly always good, and, since 1953 when we began to hold the meeting in July, sometimes warm. It will be unfortunate if we become too severely athletic and neglect this side of the sports, and the lighthearted sack races and handicap quarter-mile. For we are now taking athletics more seriously. Boys may now choose between cricket and athletics at the beginning of the summer term, knowing that in athletics they will have systematic coaching and meetings with other clubs. Yet, in spite of the rather casual approach to athletics in the past we have produced one or two first-rate F.P. track men. Both Dr. J. F. A. Wood and A.G. Blair have represented Scotland; Ivan Tait won the Scottish Amateur One Hundred Yards in 1920 and R. H. H. Wallace the quarter-mile. Appendix D gives details of records at the school sports.

The F.P. Golf Club has been in existence at least since 1892; the first minute book begins with an account of the annual general meeting of 1893. It was a small club at first, a club of twelve members with J. Rose as captain, helped on its way by the encouragement of Mr. Buchanan, the convener, who presented the Buchanan Medal and by the Athletic Club which presented the gold medal for competition. Numbers increased fast. By 1906 there were ninety members, twenty of whom were scratch players. To-day there are a hundred and sixty. This increase took place at a time when the school was not very enamoured of golf and the individualism it implies. The game was considered a dangerous enemy of cricket and, if not discouraged, at least received little encouragement until very recently. To-day the school club has a visiting professional as instructor and a full summer programme.

By 1911 the F.P. Club was firmly established and achieved its first considerable success when J. F. Mitchell, J. H. MacGregor, J. D. Little and H. J. Kerr won the *Evening Dispatch* Trophy, a victory they were to repeat in 1912. Already the club had twice won the Harvieston Trophy* and was producing players who distinguished themselves in outside competitions. In 1907 J. Douglas Brown won the Irish Open. J. F. Mitchell also won the Irish Open in 1908 after being Runner-up in 1904 and 1905 and in 1909 J. D. Little won the scratch prize in the Irish Amateur Championship, and won the South of Ireland championship. E. M. Fitzjohn, an F.P., though probably not a member of the club, had lowered the record for the Old Royal Musselburgh Course, playing with a gutty.

The club was, and is, dependent for its competitions and for its annual match against Watsonians on the use of public or private courses—Gullane, North Berwick, Elie, Bathgate, St. Andrews and others, including two, the names of which are now memories— North Queensferry and Archerfield. The secretary sometimes found that his careful arrangements were upset by members' reluctance to travel. In 1909 the October meeting at North Berwick attracted two players only.

During the 1914-18 war the club temporarily ceased but was revived again in 1919 and soon found players to represent it. In 1923 and 1924 C. Mann, A. L. Robson, A. M. Macdonald and J. C. Irving won the *Evening Dispatch* Trophy again; and in 1929 and 1947 the Stewart's team was in the final. In 1954 the club won the Queen Elizabeth Coronation Schools' Trophy with the following team—J. R. McIntosh, Dr. J. F. A. Wood, J. Burnside, J. T. Porteous Dr. T. A. White, and J. B. Pringle. Of the other golfers of this generation it will be sufficient to recall that R. A. Cruickshank was among the leaders in the U.S. Open Championship and a winner

* The Harvieston Trophy, instituted by a Gorebridge Golf Club captain, in 1898 was played for under similar conditions to the *Evening Dispatch* Trophy. The F.P. club won the Trophy in 1904 and 1905.

of big tournaments, and to remind golfers of D. Wemyss, probably the best all-round boy golfer we have had in the past twenty years, who later became a full Scottish Internationalist, Stewart's F.P. Golf Club's only one, and who is now in South Africa.

Space must be found to say a little about shooting. In the ten years from 1884 to 1894 Stewart's teams competed for the Edinburgh District Schools' Trophy with astonishing success. The test was an exacting one—seven shots at two hundred yards, kneeling and seven at five hundred lying, carried out first at the Blackford ranges and thereafter at Hunter's Bog. From 1884-88 we won this trophy each year; in 1889 and 1890 we took no part; and in 1891, 1892 and 1894 we again won. "Tiger" MacDonald was the coach, and some of the team were to carry on shooting after they left school with success: J. L. Thomson won the Queen's Prize at Bisley in 1896 and H. Ommundsen, who was killed in 1915 as a Lieutenant of the H.A.C. won the service rifle competition in 1905, 1908, 1910 and 1912.

Rugby football began in School as a playground game in the early days of the Institute. By 1872 a school club was organised and James Gibb, the captain, challenged Watson's to a match. We won that first game by a dropped goal, helped probably by Mr. Macrae of the staff who played for the first Twenty. Thereafter we met Watson's annually, our first and second Twenties against two Watson's Twenties. But we had few other fixtures till Ravelston was acquired. Then, first, a list of fixtures was drawn up and the Fifteen had an undefeated first season, playing with a team of a full back, three half backs, two quarter backs and nine forwards. One of these early players was distinguished later at Association football—A. J. Christie who later played for Queen's Park and was twice capped, in full international games, for Scotland. Jerseys were red and blue, horizontally striped, till 1896 when the new red, black and gold jerseys were introduced. With the new jerseys came the new ground at Inverleith, level ground, where the grass was cut and wily lads could no longer tie together the tops of tussocks to make snares for their opponents. There we have remained, adding to our territory the Union field in 1926 and slowly making the little cabbage patch on the south into a small junior pitch.

Inverleith has seen the great seasons, such as 1912-13, when J. M. Davie was captain of the School Fifteen and we lost one game only, a critical game, for the Fifteen had decided that if they were undefeated they would change from navy blue to white shorts. Inverleith has seen, too, a great increase in the number of our opponents. The fixture card for the season 1897-8, when James Scobie was captain, lists six opposing teams only—2nd Watson's,

3rd Loretto, 1st Royal High School and 1st Heriots, 3rd F.P. Fifteen and Moreland. The card with its many vacant Saturdays makes interesting comparison with our present one, both in the number of fixtures and in the quality of the opposition. For many seasons our 1st Fifteen School side was not considered good enough to play Watson's 1st Fifteen hence Watson's 2nd Fifteen supplied the opposition. On a Wednesday afternoon however in 1904 a game was arranged between 1st Stewart's and 1st Watson's. The result was a win for Watson's—sixteen points to eight points—quite a creditable result as the Watson's team included several boys who in later years played for Scotland. Though the standard of play improved with the increasing numbers of players in the school club, it was not till the captaincy of Maxwell Jones in 1925 that we were granted a regular fixture with Watson's 1st Fifteen. The victors still recall the tea Dr. Milne provided after the game to celebrate our win.

Inverleith has seen the number of boys playing football steadily increase. By the nineteen twenties Mr. Lyell was rejoicing in six senior and three junior teams and in the present season 1954-1955 there are eleven senior and six junior fifteens. The increase in the number of players and fixtures has meant an increase in magisterial supervision, so that to-day each team has a master to look after it, coach it and encourage it, with a master to act as club secretary and supervise generally. For long Mr. Hardie did this, and much more.

But the college club is too overshadowed by the F.P. Club for me to spend more time on it. Almost all the best of the school players join the F.P. Club and then they normally improve their playing so that the memory of the brilliant schoolboy footballer is forgotten in the present achievements of the F.P. Presumably even the boys themselves think of their place in the Fifteen not as the fruition of an earthly crown but as a stepping stone to higher things.

The F.P. Club is long established in name and longer in fact. In 1880 the Warrender Club was formed, mainly from our F.P.'s with a ground at Warrender Park and Cossar Mackenzie as captain. Other F.P.'s joined the St. George or the junior Roseneath club. When Stewart's College Athletic Club was founded the members of Warrender and Roseneath combined to form the F.P. Club bringing with them the Warrender fixture card. The St. George remained aloof and continued for a while as a separate club.

Season 1885-6 was the first football season as Stewart's College F.P. The captain was A. A. Gibb, the secretary W. C. Mackenzie, the colours Oxford Blue Jersey, Red Sash and White Shorts. (In 1886, the club (captain, W. C. Mackenzie) became a member of the Scottish Rugby Union. Since that date the club has regularly taken part in the unofficial Scottish Rugby Championship.

The first notable victory was over the Royal High School F.P. in 1889 when the Scholars lost by a try, their defeat being described at the time as being principally due to "brute force and bloody ignorance." Many well-known names in Stewart's Rugby Annals figure in the years prior to the advent of the present century—D. M. D. Yule, A. Moffatt MacDonald, Dr. Erskine, W. B. Morrison (brother of the more famous Mark Morrison). The lack of an adequate playing-field was keenly felt at this time and a movement, pioneered by the Hon. Secretary of the Club, D. H. Gordon Smith, led to the Governors of the College acquiring ground at Inverleith, to which a migration took place in 1895. That date is the second important one in the history of the Club. The change was of inestimable benefit both to the present and former pupils.

Once established in the new ground we enjoyed a period of greater prosperity and a feature of those days was the keen rivalry existing between Stewart's and Heriot's. The Club had a reputation for good forwards—a reputation which it has never lost—and goal-dropping centre-threes, but an up-to-date style of "back" play was difficult to cultivate. The seasons passed and we met with varied fortunes, never being champions but always acquiring the name of "spoilers," a name we have never lost. In 1910, J. G. Bell, our full back, came into prominence and was fancied as a candidate for a place in the Scottish side. He chose, however, when he played for his native Carlisle to aspire to English International honours but never secured a "Cap" although he was a reserve for England.

In 1911-12 we had a grand pack led by Finlay Kennedy and including G. M. Beaton, J. D. Lunan and W. L. Kerr. Kennedy's play and personality were an inspiration to the team and when T. Russell Tod, Ivan Tait and J. A. Mann came into the back division we were a well-balanced side. Many of the 1913-1914 players were killed in the First Great War.

The war stopped matches for a while and Rugby was no resumed until 1919. Kennedy returned to the side and he and Dr. J. C. R. Buchanan played in the Inter-City match in season 1919-20 and Kennedy went on to play for Scotland against England, Ireland, Wales and France, thus gaining the distinction of being the first Stewart's College Internationalist. Kennedy's death, a few years later, was a great shock, not only to Stewart's, but to all followers of the game. He will be long remembered for his feat in the first post-war Welsh International at Inverleith, February

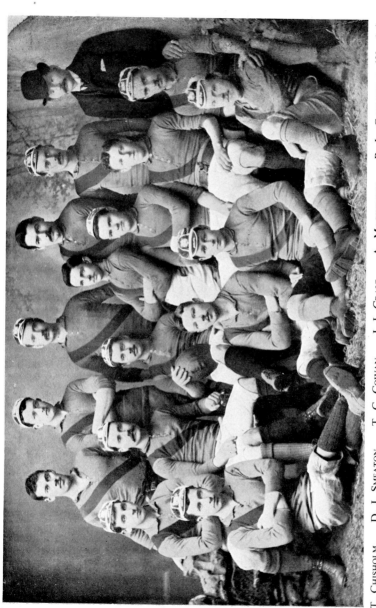

T. CHISHOLM.   D. J. SMEATON.   T. C. COWAN.   J. I. CRAIG.   A. MACKENZIE.   R. L. GALLOWAY. (*Umpire*).
G. R. TURNER.   C. M. GIBB.   W. C. MACKENZIE (*Captain*).   J. DICK.   J. M. GOW.   D. SMITH.   L. P. MACKENZIE.
J. A. TURNER.   J. M. WILSON.   F. D. CAMERON.   J. ROSE.

1920—two magnificent penalty goals which he kicked from beyond the centre line, ten yards in from touch in front of the Press box, so enabling Scotland to win by nine points to five. His kicking inspired Henri Meslier:—

> C'est son talent qui valut la victoire:
> Louons la force de son coup de pied.
> De Stewart's College il ajoute à la gloire
> Kennedy! Kennedy! Kennedy!

In April 1920 Stewart's College F.P. won the Edinburgh Sevens and the Melrose Cup (Sevens) with I. Tait, R. Tod, C. V. Hendry, J. A. Mann, F. Kennedy, J. C. R. Buchanan, A. D. Lambert; and later Sevens have been successful at all Border and Edinburgh sports.

Season 1920-21 was one of the best that the Club ever had. We went undefeated until New Year's Day, finishing the season with thirteen wins, four defeats and two draws—a record which enabled us, along with Hawick and Glasgow High School, to take second place to Watsonians. The backs of that side included T. R. Tod, Ivan Tait, S. M. Thomson, G. I. Stewart, J. J. Mann at full back and C. V. Hendry and J. A. Mann at half. The forwards included Kennedy, J. C. R. Buchanan, A. D. Lambert and J. T. Macpherson. That season Buchanan and Kennedy gained International honours.

In season 1925-26 the Club led by J. W. Scott, our third Internationalist, was the second best Edinburgh Club, winning eleven matches, losing five and drawing two. The "capping" of Jumbo Scott maintained the Club's record of having had a representative capped every year since the war. We had also never been without a player in post-war Inter-City matches. The players so honoured, in addition to Kennedy, Tait and Buchanan, were Scott, J. J. Mann, A. D. Lambert, S. M. Thomson, H. P. Mather and A. Lovat Fraser.

The third most important date in the history of the Club was 1926 when the Scottish Rugby Union Ground at Inverleith became the headquarters of Stewart's College Rugby. The existing playing and dressing accommodation had become inadequate for the growing needs of both P.P.'s and F.P.'s and the Merchant Company with support and aid of the Club—President John Hay, Secretary T. D. Adie—purchased the S.R.U. ground which had been superseded by Murrayfield as the venue of International matches. It was said then that the possession of the best-equipped and largest ground in the country would be an incentive to Stewart's Former Pupils to surpass anything which the Club had yet accomplished on the rugby field. How true these words proved to be!

The season 1934-35 proved to be a very successful one in the Club's history. Along with Glasgow University we finished "runners-up" to Watsonians in the Club Championship. We won more games (twenty-three) and secured more points (four hundred and three) than any other senior club in Scotland. It was a sore point with us that we lost the Championship that year, for the side included so many brilliant players. We provided five of Edinburgh's Fifteen against Glasgow in the Inter-City and the same afternoon suffered by having our first defeat; Edinburgh Wanderers beating our much weakened side.

Incidentally, the total of four hundred and three points scored was a record for the Club, being made up of eighty-seven tries, thirty conversions, eighteen penalty goals and seven drop goals. Of this total A. G. Blair contributed no fewer than one hundred and fifty-five points amassed from twenty tries, twenty-five goal kicks and fifteen penalties—surely an individual record that will stand for many years to come.

Whatever arguments there may have been that year, however, there was no doubt about our success in 1937-38 when at last we achieved our ambition of winning the Championship. The side may not have shown the brilliance which shone at times in the 1934-35 team, but the pack was solid, quick heeling and quick breaking and the backs reliable and more consistent than in the past. The players who brought this honour to the Club were:—
P. H. Hyslop, A. G. Blair, J. K. Tait, J. Irvine, J. S. Drummond, A. E. Bennett, L. G. Doig, E. Anderson, J. B. Borthwick, A. D. Govan, H. B. Johnson, J. Craig, W. F. Malcolm, J. Kelly, J. R. Kyles and D. J. Epworth. The record for the season was:—

P.	W.	L.	D.	Pts. For	Pts. Agst.
20	16	3	1	263	154

A. G. Blair was again the principal contributor to this total with one hundred twenty-four points from twelve tries, eighteen conversions, sixteen penalties and one drop goal. A. V. Scott was President of the Club and not a little of its success was due to his enthusiasm and judgement.

The following season was full of promise and with some good young replacements for the "veterans," prospects looked decidedly bright, but before season 1939-40 had started war was upon us and the next six years were difficult days indeed. All normal club arrangements were cancelled and a new fixture card for one Fifteen only was arranged. Membership fell steadily during the season as players were called up for National Service but, notwithstanding our difficulties, the Club made history with the fine record of fifteen games played without defeat, scoring two hundred and ninety-six points against seventy-two. For a short time in 1940-41 we ran two teams, the 1st Fifteen again playing well despite the inclusion of inexperienced players, and finished the season with twelve wins out of seventeen games played. In the third wartime season it seemed doubtful if the Club could carry on as most of the office-bearers were now on active service but it was felt by those who were left that it would be in the future interests of the Club to struggle on even with a playing strength as low as seventeen so that there would at least be the nucleus of a team when happier days returned. And so for the next four years the Club carried on, at times only with the help of old players on leave or "guest" players from service units in the district, but at least keeping the Club in being. In all, one hundred and seven games were played of which fifty-eight were won, forty-four lost and five drawn. The early success of the Club when normal rugby was resumed after the war could perhaps be attributed to the continuity which had been maintained during the war years through the faithful service of its President, A. L. Fraser, and its Secretary, A. B. Kinnear, assisted by J. Yorston as referee and the enthusiasm of A. E. Bennett and R. L. Sharp as players throughout this period.

1945-46 saw rugby fixtures being resumed on normal lines, and with the gradual return of players from the Forces, Stewart's F.P. again began to be a club to be regarded with no little respect. In the next season, under the captaincy of Lex Govan who had been captain at the outbreak of war, the 1st Fifteen, including many of the players of seven years before, won the Championship for the second time in the Club's history. Their Championship record was:—

P.	W.	L.	D.	Pts. For	Pts. Agst.
17	16	1	0	227	21

and the complete fixture card showed:—

21	19	2	0	295	41

The only Championship defeat was at the hands of Glasgow High School F.P. by the margin of a dropped goal scored in the last minutes of a very evenly contested game. A feature of the play of this team was its strong defence, our line being crossed on only four occasions in the Championship and six times in all games played, probably a record in Scottish Rugby. The total points scored were made up of sixty-five tries (twenty-one by forwards, forty-four by backs) twenty-five conversions, eight drop goals and six penalties, the small number of penalty goals being of interest in these days when they figure so largely in club results. The team was:—P. H. Hyslop, A. E. Bennett, J. B. Pringle, J. K. Tait, J. M. Baird, W. MacLennan, J. W. C. Foubister, E. Anderson, S. T. H. Wright, A. D. Govan, W. S. Gillam, J. Craig, S. G. C. Govan, J. R. Kyles, R. Koren and R. L. Sharp.

It was perhaps fitting that in this season the Club should make further history in that Ernie Anderson became the first Stewart's back to be capped for Scotland, playing against both Ireland and England.

The following season was almost as successful for the club and we finished as runners-up to Kelso in the Championship suffering only four defeats in twenty-three games. This season was notable for our first visit to Belfast to play Instonians and North of Ireland, and we made history again by being the first club side to travel by air to fulfil a fixture! The team was much the same as the previous year, but Rolf Koren's presence was now making itself very much felt and in him and Ernie Anderson, who captained the side, the Club had two of the personalities of Scottish Rugby.

E. Anderson again led the team in 1948-49 and although the veterans, Albert Bennett and Jim Craig, had now "hung up their boots" the younger players who came into the team well maintained the high standard set by the Club in the post-war years. Again we finished as runners-up, this time to Hawick, losing four games out of twenty-three played in the Championship and had it not been for injuries which deprived us of the services of J. W. C. Foubister, J. B. Pringle and C. Ross for part of the season we might well have come out on top once more. As it was, we had the satisfaction of defeating Hawick at their own ground by nine points to nil—the only home defeat suffered by the Champions that year. In the International field the Club was honoured by the "capping" of S. T. H. Wright against England.

These three immediate post-war seasons were without doubt the best in the history of the Club. In championship games our record was:—

P.	W.	L.	D.	Pts. For	Pts. Agst.
63	48	9	6	750	220

a record which no other club could equal!

With the retiral of more of the old campaigners season 1949-50 showed a slight recession in form but the Club still finished in the top half dozen in the Championship, a position well maintained through 1950-51 and 1951-52. In 1952-53 an unfortunate injury to E. Anderson in the opening game necessitated his retirement from the game and Scottish Rugby lost one of its few real personalities since the war. The Club felt the loss of his leadership and experience very much and finished the season in a rather lower position than we had been accustomed to, and the following year we fell further when injuries and team building difficulties hit us unusually hard. After the Irish Tour at the end of December, however, a new spirit entered the team and by the end of the season they had managed to record as many wins as they had sustained losses. Grant Weatherstone who had received his first "cap" against England in 1952 and played against Ireland and England the following year played in all five International Matches in 1954.

And so we come to the present season which promises to be another outstanding one. The team built up last year with so many setbacks has proved itself almost unbeatable, and has provided no fewer than eight players to representative and trial games while for the first time in thirty years two players, T. G. Weatherstone and W. K. L. Relph, the captain and vice-captain, have been chosen for the Scottish team. Despite the demands of district games and the incidence of injuries which have forced the team to play with several reserves practically every Saturday, the Club is at present heading the Championship. As almost all the members of the team played for the School Fifteen in the post-war period some of its success is due to the revival of school rugby in the period, a revival due both to enthusiastic coaching and to such captains as Grant Weatherstone and Ian Forbes.

INVERLEITH II

HE F.P. Cricket Club was founded in 1887, a branch of the Stewart's College Athletic Club, not a very healthy branch apparently, for there are references to a "revival" in 1893. But after we got Inverleith it began to grow with fresh vigour. Some of the notable players of Ravelston days were T. Cowan, the captain in 1887, R. W. Elder, the captain from 1890 to 1896, A. D. Brownless, W. L. Lindsay, G. W. Morris, J. K. Pratt, D. Smeaton, D. Smith and G. R. Turner. David Smith, who was secretary in 1889 and captain in 1897 and 1898, had the reputation of being a specially fast bowler. He did much for the Club till business took him to Leeds.

A first impression of Inverleith about 1900 was that it was bounded on the east by a high black sleeper fence merging into a thick hedge pierced by a small wicket gate just behind the pavilion, this being our only communication to Union Field. The cinder paths were not yet and there was a strip of long grass about fifteen feet wide from the Ferry Road to the Pavilion. Then extending westwards from the pavilion towards Fettes Avenue was a high wire netting fence enclosing nursery ground, there also being a nursery over the wall which was our western boundary and which was removed quite recently for the easier working of our field and that of the Mary Erskine School. Then on the Ferry Road side, about half way along, was a thatched cottage with board fencing around, and many and violent were the discussions when the tenants were disturbed, with near pandemonium when a ball carried into the garden. Our groundsman's house was the upper storey of the pavilion until 1926 when Union Field was acquired, along with Inverleith Cottage which stood immediately below the present pay boxes until it was demolished about 1938 in the widening of the Ferry Road, which also took a strip of over eighteen feet from our playing area. The pavilion, which has surely given us splendid service for sixty years, was originally only about half its present size; the baths and the south half of the visitors' room, were added prior to 1914.

In these days the only cricket boundaries were the walls and fences and the cinders in front of the pavilion so that batsmen and fielders had much more running than now. There was one occasion at least when the batsmen ran five for a leg hit to the pavilion which if it had travelled two feet more on to the cinders would have qualified as a four boundary and saved the fielders much toil and worry.

A press report of 1897 states that in reply to our score of ninety-eight the opposition had scored eighty-six for nine just on seven o'clock and that the last batsman when nearly at the wicket was recalled by his captain. On observing this the Stewart's captain went to the pavilion to persuade his vis-a-vis to continue the over of which only one ball had been bowled. "The visiting captain was obdurate however and after fifteen minutes discussion the game was left drawn."

In early Inverleith times it was not unknown for the 1st and 2nd Elevens to be at home the same afternoon and delays while fielders sprinted through the other games were quite common. Another item of interest was that the wickets were pitched east and west instead of north and south as at present and many were the heated arguments before the change was made. It was ultimately decided that the westering sun played too big a part in our matches —almost invariably the fast bowler was put on at the top end with the sun behind his arm, and batting was accordingly quite a task, even more so when the bowler's shadow lengthened down the wicket.

Early Inverleith notables in addition to those who continued from Ravelston included A. J. J. Brown (captain 1906) H. W. R. Davidson, Rev. D. W. Inglis (captain 1899 and 1903), J. M. Inglis, A. M., A. S. and F. W. Johnston—three of a remarkable brotherhood of five who were all plus or scratch golfers—A. Macmeikan, H. B. Melville (captain 1900-01) J. J. Ross (captain 1902-03), J. Scobie (captain 1904-05) and R. Young. It is pleasing to see that A. Macmeikan, a very sound bat in the 1904-05 Elevens, and the secretary in 1906, is still a frequent visitor to Inverleith. Special mention should be made of Peter Bell, our groundsman from 1895 till his death in 1915. An F.P. himself, his main theme in sport, summer and winter, was that Stewart's would come out on top or thereabouts, and no matter how black the outlook or the score he was always full of the view that we would "nail them in the second half." He played in the F.P. Eleven for about ten years and captured many wickets. Bowling was his forte but perhaps his happiest memory was of scoring a hearty (but unorthodox) fifty-five in our first ever defeat of the Grange in 1904. One of his dearest wishes, not to be realised in his time, alas, was to see us victorious over the Watsonians at cricket and football. Old timers will recall his most succulent and large penny fruit cakes which definitely contained fruit.

Many will remember that clubs such as ours used to engage a playing professional, and our earliest contract is still extant which states that at the rate of £2, 2s. per week, our professional was to coach the boys at school every afternoon, to coach the F.P.'s in the evenings (one evening a week excepted), to play in all F.P. matches, to assist the groundsman, especially in cutting, preparing and rolling wickets. In addition he was told: "As you will be well aware, there are other minor duties incidental to the work of all professionals." It seems obvious that with board and lodging to be met from wages our professional would not be unduly affluent, or have much, if any, spare time, but in fact we obtained many excellent cricketers from the south. The first of these, E. J. Newton, had played with distinction for his county and was quite outstanding, his coaching and experience being of the greatest value to our cricket. The F.P. Club ceased to employ a professional on its own account in 1913.

Jas. Scobie commenced about 1899, a notable connection of two sets of brothers—Scobies and Turnbulls—whose ages were such that as opening batsmen and bowlers they inevitably appear prominently in the records over a long period, the playing service alone extending up to 1939. Their times also included much official service, J. B. Turnbull for instance having three spells of captaincy, covering nine seasons in all.

Apart from these recruits many fine cricketers were coming forward and the prowess and status of the Club steadily increased from about 1905 to the 1920's when it could claim to rank with the best in Scotland. In 1919 first victories were obtained over Royal High School and Edinburgh Academicals, while from the beginning of August 1922 to the end of June 1924, only one match was lost— by twenty-four runs. As regards both paper results and cricket abilities the best season was 1923 when eighteen matches were played of which twelve were won, five drawn and one lost. The Official Eleven (alphabetically) was J. A. T. Brown, I. G. Morrison, N. Nisbet, C. C. Robson, S. F. St. Clair, W. M., A., and C. S. Scobie, W. F. and J. B. Turnbull, and W. K. White. J. F. C. Hogg, J. J. Finlay and L. S. Kinnear also appeared with distinction. Each and every one could, and did, play a notable part at some time or other but teamwork was an outstanding feature with, perhaps best of all, fielding and catching of an unusually high standard. J. A. T. Brown (captain 1932-35, 1938 and 1946) and I. G. Morrison (captain 1936) were both up and coming youngsters destined to play big parts in later years; N. Nisbet (captain 1923-24) was an able captain, a sound batsman and a magnificent catch; C. C. Robson (captain 1919, 1922, and 1927) was a most competent and free-scoring batsman whose style and strokes were worthy of imitation by any youngster, and an outstanding cover point for

[*Ayton.*

R. MacNeill.   D. J. Smeaton.   T. W. Morris.   Bell (*Prof*).

A. D. Brownlees.   D. W. Inglis.   R. W. Hepburn.   D. Smith.
R. W. Elder (*Captain*).   J. Shields.   J. Jeffrey.   T. Sellars.

many years, during which his fielding received frequent commendation in the records. He was, it seems, the only boy to score a century for the School 1st Eleven, and just failed (ninety-eight against Heriot's in 1921) to score one for the F.P.'s too. S. F. St. Clair (captain 1928) though sometimes a quietish starter was another hard-hitting fast-scoring batsman over many seasons; W. K. R. White (captain 1925-26 and 1931) was our wicket-keeper and, when set, yet another attractive fast-scoring batsman. A memory flash is his stumping appeal, to an umpire whose mind one fears had strayed, answered in the negative when, quick as thought and seeing the batsman was still from home, a stump was snatched up according to rule with another confident appeal—also answered, alas in the negative. Loud comment from local supporter—"O aye, gi'e him a' the wickets tae play wi'". J. F. C. Hogg and J. J. Finlay were very effective fast bowlers, and L. S. Kinnear was a mighty hitter and a mighty fielder too.

From 1930 onwards playing results were less successful, particularly as regards run getting and more particularly as regards the first fifty to one hundred, which had presented little difficulty in the purple periods, and was frequently achieved for the first wicket. Many good performances were put up however, and the club continued in good health. J. A. T. Brown and I. G. Morrison amply fulfilled their earlier promise and notable recruits came along in J. B. Anderstrem, R. O. Haywood, (captain 1937), H. P. Mather (captain 1939), F. E. O'Riordan, A. V. Plowright and A. A. Williamson (captain 1950-53), each and all of whom have made many notable contributions.

In the post-war period further personalities appeared in J. W. C. Foubister (captain 1954), E. Hyndman, A. G. Mackay and S. T. H. Wright and in the ordinary course all of these will continue to figure prominently in the Club records.

The most prolific scorer for the Club was W. F. Turnbull, who on many occasions headed the club batting averages, even, one year, the Scottish averages. His highest club total was 959 runs in 1913 with an average of 73.76 per innings; in all matches he exceeded 1000 runs in this and other seasons. He scored many centuries, one press report making special mention of 105 not out in eighty-five minutes (against Edinburgh Academicals 1920) out of 134 for 2 wickets, the other three batsmen only having time and opportunity to score 27 in all and Extras 2. He played for Scotland on several occasions and the records mention his refusal of further honours for business reasons.

Other members who have played for Scotland are R. O. Haywood, A. V. Plowright, A. E. Sellars, and C. S. Scobie plus of course

R. H. E. Chisholm from Aberdeenshire, whose appointment to the School Staff in 1954 will mean much to our cricket. A. E. Sellars played mainly for Leith Caledonian and Carlton, while C. S. Scobie latterly played for Grange. Other century makers include J. A. T. Brown against Leith Franklin, R. O. Haywood against Murrayfield and Melville F.P., S. F. St. Clair against Grange and W. K. R. White against our School Eleven. Special reference must be made to R. O. Haywood's 102 against Melville F.P. at Ferryfield in 1951 in less than an hour, including no fewer than 8 sixes and 7 fours. A hurricane indeed.

With much longer boundaries, sixes were scarce at Inverleith in the early days, but one recalls a huge hit by L. S. Kinnear into the nursery off a fast bowler in our first ever win over Watsonians in 1923. From the south end the writer can only recall one by S. F. St. Clair into the Ferry Road, and one by J. Nichol, Heriot's, in 1921 into Ferryfield via the Ferry Road. Another pleasant memory is of two enormous sixes by E. Hyndman from the bottom end at Myreside, the second clearing the back fence in front of the pavilion.

The highest 1st Eleven total is 265 for 8 against Grange in 1930, while 250 for 3 was scored against Heriot's in 1905. In 1924 an unusual record was achieved against Leith Franklin when after two hours twenty minutes batting and without the loss of a wicket our innings was closed at 204. (W. F. Turnbull not out 116, J. B. Turnbull not out 81, Byes 5, No Balls 2.) W. Finlay Gordon (a most promising batsman who met a tragically early death) and W. F. Turnbull also topped the 200 on an earlier occasion before being separated.

The highest scoring game and one of the most exhilarating and sporting encounters was that against Grange in 1919 at Raeburn Place. Each side had two and a quarter hours batting and in reply to the Grange total of 237 for 7, we scored 232 for 4—almost an ideal draw. Another high scoring game was in 1913 when Selkirk, in reply to our 257 for 8 scored 199 for 5. The lowest score recorded is 35 against St. Boswell's in 1924, in response to which we shot our opponents out for 23! Over the last twenty-five years J. A. T. Brown has been the most remarkably consistent performer both in batting and bowling. He has headed the averages on many occasions and even in 1954 we find him achieving a hat-trick at Penicuik.

The most successful and consistent bowler in the period between the wars was A. Scobie. From 1923 when he took up bowling seriously (he was previously an opening bat on occasion) up to 1939 he took about seven hundred wickets, generally at very low cost. His biggest bag was 61 wickets in 1933 for 8.8 runs each, and his most remarkable effort, which is unlikely to be surpassed or even equalled in any club, was in 1932 when he took 7 wickets for 0 runs against Hillhead High School F.P. at Inverleith in 7.5 overs. (Our opponents were all out for 11, I. D. Watson taking 3 wickets for 7, the balance being a four bye.) There is no record of a 1st Eleven bowler taking all 10 wickets, though W. M. Scobie accomplished this in a 2nd Eleven game. J. A. T. Brown took 9 for 25 against Edinburgh University in 1923, and Andrew Turnbull had 9 for 69 against Stenhousemuir in 1910. It is interesting that on each of these occasions the bowler took the first nine wickets and was denied the last. The records also mention specially J. B. Turnbull's 8 for 20 against Leith Franklin (1930), and 6 for 11 against Hawick (1923), C. S. Scobie 7 for 12 against St. Boswells (1924) and A. V. Plowright 6 for 8 against West Lothian County (1939).

Apart from mere figures however, mention should be made of J. B. Anderstrem, a really first-class bowler, who too often has had to bear too much of the heat and burden of the day, and who has, for that reason, so often bowled very much better than his figures show.

Hat tricks have been comparatively scarce, especially in the earlier years. J. A. T. Brown has had at least three against Kirkcaldy, Brunswick and Penicuik; J. Scobie had one against Berwick; J. F. C. Hogg against Watsonians; F. L. Pool against Edinburgh Academicals; and H. G. McCall against Glasgow High School F.P. Perhaps the most dramatic was that of J. F. C. Hogg who clean bowled all his victims and these were no mean batsmen.

Wicket-keepers included R. Young whose scholastic duties, however, took him about 1900 to Fifeshire, for whom he kept for many years, and we seem to recall him playing for a Scottish representative side—he was certainly of that standard; H. D'Arcy Barker (captain 1907) who also did a very great deal for the club behind the scenes; W. K. R. White already mentioned; and R. Smith (captain 1947-49) whose many valuable services included the gift of a concrete practice wicket.

Left handers have been remarkably few, in sixty years the most prominent being two all rounders, Andrew Turnbull, M. Gravett, one of our four professionals, and D. R. S. McIntosh, a successful bowler just prior to the war.

Tribute must be paid here to the great services of Ian D. Watson, who in addition to playing, acted as Honorary Secretary and Treasurer from 1927 until his death in 1948. Suitable appreciation was expressed, and the presentation of a wireless set made, at the Jubilee Dinner held in 1947.

At the time of writing the President of the Club is Mr. James

Black, who has given much valuable service in that office since 1951, and has in addition umpired nearly all the 1st Eleven matches in that time. The Honorary Secretary and Treasurer since 1952 has been Mr. K. T. Waite.

Unfortunately space does not permit the mention of the many, many others, the great majority, who are in so many ways the essential ingredient of any club for their constancy and camaraderie. But one must refer to J. B. Wilton, a colourful personality for forty years. The anecdotes about J. B. are endless, and few who met him will forget him and his phenomenal keenness for cricket, or his enormous bag always packed ready to travel anywhere, at almost any notice. Peace to his ashes!

EPILOGUE

AND so the story is told. I am conscious that it is not complete in many ways, especially I regret that it has not been possible to find out more about the founder. Others will miss the events and people they expected to find, or will criticise the little attention given to what they judge important. But any history, if it is to be readable, must be a record of what matters, not merely of what happened: and ultimately the writer must decide what matters. It can never be objective. Above all a work of this kind, where so much of the evidence was oral and made vivid by the enthusiasm of the witnesses cannot be objective. I have tried to set out what appear to be the important things of a century of growth from the hospital with its handful of foundationers to the public school of some eight hundred boys, and I suppose that I have tried to explain the present boy in terms of the society which has helped to make him and the society in terms of the boy.

We make whole men, or try to make them, failing sometimes from the flaws in the boy, or his home, or ourselves, but not losing sight of the end. We have nearly all our boys from the age of five (few other schools have them so long) and we might stamp them in one mould, identical in speech, tastes and shibboleths as so many schools do. But we have never tried to do that, and, I hope, never will. Our best are identical in these ways only—that they are Christian; that they learn to distinguish right from wrong and to prefer right; that they are adequately learned, have begun to work independently and are endowed with saving commonsense; that their bodies are matched to their minds; and that they are not boorish. In other things our toleration permits a great diversity: there is room for all kinds of heretics. These are not original virtues, but they are worth setting down, for they link us to our past. Toleration apart, they are the qualities we have aimed at in Scotland for nearly four hundred years. We have never inculcated the team (or herd) spirit; our underlying presumption in education, as in life, has been that at the end each man must find his own way home. We have preserved, too, a democratic fraternity in our society because we have avoided a caste system of education and have kept our regional tongues. There are very few schools left in Scotland like us. We have the freedom to experiment and do what seems wisest to us; we do not have to conform to the administrative requirements of an Education Authority; we are grant-aided and our doors are, therefore, open to most; and we are utterly Scottish, preserving the traditions which have formed us as a nation. For a century we have sent out a flow of men to enrich the nation and to be examples to this and future generations of boys. We may hope that our generation and its successors will permit my successor a hundred years hence to chronicle an even greater century.

"Ite nunc fortes ubi celsa magni
Ducit exempli via"

1955

SPACE MEN OF CLASS 2B.

[N. *Inglis.*

APPENDIX A.

NUMBERS IN SCHOOL

1870–81	.... *approx.*	300	1917–18	....	500
1881–82	....	312	1918–19	....	512
1882–83	....	439	1919–20	....	521
1883–84	....	569	1920–21	....	517
1884–85	....	689	1921–22	....	566
1885–86	....	740	1922–23	....	571
1886–87	....	814	1923–24	....	588
1887–88	....	871	1924–25	....	587
1888–89	....	874	1925–26	....	637
1889–90	....	890	1926–27	....	646
1890–91	....	843	1927–28	....	636
1891–92	....	837	1928–29	....	646
1892–93	....	786	1929–30	....	671
1893–94	....	675	1930–31	....	686
1894–95	....	681	1931–32	....	686
1895–96	....	697	1932–33	....	681
1896–97	....	676	1933–34	....	673
1897–98	....	639	1934–35	....	689
1898–99	....	609	1935–36	....	677
1899–1900	....	562	1936–37	....	666
1900–01	....	552	1937–38	....	669
1901–02	....	556	1938–39	....	657
1902–03	....	586	1939–40	....	570
1903–04	....	572	1940–41	....	578
1904–05	....	573	1941–42	....	608
1905–06	....	553	1942–43	....	653
1906–07	....	530	1943–44	....	668
1907–08	....	538	1944–45	....	674
1908–09	....	542	1945–46	....	665
1909–10	....	541	1946–47	....	675
1910–11	....	531	1947–48	....	702
1911–12	....	494	1948–49	....	743
1912–13	....	491	1949–50	....	741
1913–14	....	484	1950–51	....	739
1914–15	....	457	1951–52	....	764
1915–16	....	466	1952–53	....	803
1916–17	....	481	1953–54	....	839

APPENDIX B.

OCCUPATIONS OF FATHERS IN 1893

Merchants	227
Clergy	11
Lawyers and C.A.'s	29
Farmers	34
Medical Practitioners	6
Bankers and Insurance Agents	29
Civil Servants and Officers of the Army and Navy	42
Clerks in Lawyer's Offices and Commercial Houses	29
Teachers	22
Commercial Travellers	45
Builders, Contractors and Architects	33
Managers of Works	41
Engineers	13
Artists	9
Journalists	4
Railway Officials	9
Printers and Publishers	19
Hoteliers	13
Manufacturers	15
Not Classified	30
Deceased	100
	760

This is from a report of the Headmaster to the Governors.

APPENDIX B2.

OCCUPATIONS OF FATHERS IN 1931

MERCHANTS	190
CLERKS, COMMERCIAL TRAVELLERS, ETC.	104
ARCHITECTS	8
C.A.'s	4
INSURANCE	14
BANK	17
MINISTERS	13
TEACHERS	13
DOCTORS AND DENTISTS	13
CIVIL SERVICE, INCLUDING G.P.O.	63
LAW	19
ENGINEERS	38
RAILWAY	3
SEA	26
CORPORATION SERVANTS	7
NEWSPAPER—PRESS	4
FARMERS	12
WIDOWS	42
BOTH PARENTS DEAD	0
TOTAL	590

APPENDIX C

LIST OF MASTERS OF THE MERCHANT COMPANY SINCE 1855 AND OF THE VICE-CONVENERS OF DANIEL STEWART'S COLLEGE

MASTERS

1855	JAMES CRAIG
1856	CHARLES LAWSON
1857	JAMES RICHARDSON
1858	ROBERT CHAMBERS
1859	CHARLES COWAN
1860	GEORGE LORIMER
1861	CHARLES LAWSON
1862	HUGH ROSE
1863	JAMES BLACKADDER
1865	JAMES S. DUNCAN
1868	SIR THOMAS J. BOYD
1871	THOMAS KNOX
1872	JOHN CLAPPERTON
1874	ROBERT BRYSON
1877	DAVID DICKSON
1879	SIR JAMES FALSHAW, BART.
1881	JOSIAH LIVINGSTON
1883	SIR THOMAS CLARK, BART.
1885	ROBERT YOUNGER
1886	JOHN GIFFORD
1888	SIR ANDREW M'DONALD
1890	FRANCIS BLACK
1891	J. TURNBULL SMITH
1893	JOHN HERDMAN
1895	W. W. ROBERTSON
1897	ROBERT WEIR
1899	JOHN MACMILLAN
1901	ROBERT WEIR
1901	SIR JOHN COWAN, D.L., LL.D.
1903	JOHN HARRISON, LL.D.
1905	WILLIAM GRANT
1907	JAMES L. EWING, LL.D.
1910	GEORGE LORIMER
1911	SIR JOHN M. CLARK, BART.
1913	SIR JOHN R. FINDLAY, BART., K.B.E., D.L., LL.D.
1915	W. FRASER DOBIE
1917	ALEXANDER DARLING, LL.D.
1919	ANDREW HENDERSON
1921	SIR MALCOLM SMITH, K.B.E., M.P.
1922	J. W. SHENNAN
1924	MICHAEL A. T. THOMSON
1926	CHARLES W. ALLAN
1928	W. STEWART MORTON
1930	SIR GILBERT ARCHER
1932	ANDREW WILSON, O.B.E., D.L.
1934	R. H. MUNRO
1936	WILLIAM KINLOCH ANDERSON
1938	JOHN G. GALLOWAY*
1940	D. W. PENTLAND*
1941	JOHN L. WHITE, C.B.E., D.L.
1943	JOHN S. BLAIR
1945	WILLIAM TURNER EWING, D.S.O.
1947	WILLIAM DRUMMOND, C.B.E., M.C., D.L.
1949	IVER R. S. SALVESEN, T.D.
1951	ANDREW DICK WOOD
1953	STANLEY BENNET

VICE-CONVENERS

1909	D. F. WISHART
1911	JOHN WATHERSTON
1912	REV. THOMAS BURNS, D.D.
1913	SOMMERVILLE GRIEVE
1914	JAMES GALLOWAY
1915	WILLIAM INMAN
1917	ANDREW R. DRYBURGH
1918	THOMAS FERGUSON
1920	MICHAEL A. T. THOMSON
1922	J. FAIRBAIRN, JUN.*
1924	T. KERSHAW BONNAR*
1926	SIR GILBERT ARCHER
1928	JOHN G. GALLOWAY*
1930	GEORGE C. DUFF
1931	JOHN S. BLAIR
1934	J. C. SMITH
1936	SIR HUGH ROSE, BART.
1937	DAVID W. PENTLAND*
1938	A. S. HARDIE
1940	H. WALKER RUSSELL
1941	JAMES ROSS
1943	A. E. C. STEVENSON
1944	GEORGE DOBSON
1947	JAMES KENNEDY
1949	ALEXANDER WILKIE*
1950	R. N. PENTLAND (acting)
1951	JOHN M. ARCHER
1953	A. V. SCOTT*

The names marked with asterisks are those of former pupils.

APPENDIX D.

SCHOOL RECORDS

Throwing the Cricket Ball

Distance.
112 yards   E. A. USMAR

Year
1897

High Jump

Height
5 ft. 5 ins.   J. F. A. WOOD   1923

Putting the Shot

Distance
35 ft.   (14 lb.) J. GRAHAM   1929
36 ft. 11 ins.   (12 lb.) K. R. MACDONALD   1951

Long Jump

Distance
21 ft. 2 ins.   J. F. A. WOOD   1924

Quarter Mile

Time
$52\frac{1}{2}$ secs.   J. M. DAVIE   1912

100 Yards

Time
$10\frac{2}{5}$ secs.   R. A. CRUICKSHANK   1912

Mile

Time
4 min. $52\frac{1}{5}$ sec.s   J. YORSTON   1928

120 Yards Hurdles

Time
$16\frac{3}{5}$ secs.   J. F. A. WOOD   1923

Half-Mile

Time
2 min. 8 secs.   G. V. CHESTER   1946

220 Yards

Time
24 secs.   G. V. CHESTER   1945

H

APPENDIX E.

DUXES 1870–1954

AND THEIR LATER OCCUPATIONS

1870–71	Archibald Torrance	....
1871–72	Thomas Low	....
1872–73	{ William Welsh	
	{ Walter O. Walker	Medical Practitioner
1873–74	James B. Simpson	Schoolmaster
1874–75	Robert Law	Professor of New Testament Literature, Ontario
1875–76	James Rousseau	Colonial Service, Warden of Tobago
1876–77	John Somerville	
1877–78	Robert Allardice	Professor of Mathematics, Stanford University
1878–79	Robert L. Galloway	Medical Practitioner
1879–80	David Dougal	Writer to the Signet
1880–81	Peter S. Warden	C.A. in Rhodesia and Town Clerk of Salisbury
1881–82	Charles Ramage	Dental Surgeon in U.S.A.
1882–83	George M. Gibb	Minister
1883–84	Benchara B. P. Branford	L.C.C. Inspector of Schools
1884–85	James I. Craig	Financial Adviser to Egyptian Government.
1885–86	Henry Barker	Lecturer in Edinburgh University
1886–87	James S. Cairncross	Dentist
1887–88	Thomas McVey	
1888–89	William W. McKechnie	Secretary of the Scottish Education Department
1889–90	Francis Dewar	Indian Civil Service
1890–91	Arthur H. Firth	Medical Practitioner
1891–92	Peter Thomsen	Schoolmaster
1892–93	John W. Stewart	
1893–94	Andrew M. Anderson	Missionary Nyasaland & Tanganyika
1894–95	James W. Meldrum	M.A.
1895–96	John A. Ferguson	Indian Civil Service
1896–97	David C. Davidson	Missionary in Mukden
1897–98	Walter B. Gravely	Indian Civil Service, Governor of Burma.
1898–99	John Liddell Geddie	Editor of *Chambers's Journal*, etc.
1899–1900	John C. McKenzie	Indian Civil Service
1900–01	Thomas White	Indian Civil Service
1901–02	William M. Smail	Professor of Classics in Cape Town Rector of Perth Academy
1902–03	Edwin E. Todd	Soldier, Retired as Brigadier
1903–04	William S. Baxter	Schoolmaster
1904–05	{ Walter S. Clark	
	{ William Hendry	Director of Public Instruction, Zanzibar
1905–06	John S. Jolly	Assistant Librarian of Royal Scottish Museum (killed in action)
1906–07	Thomas G. Ironside	Schoolmaster

1907–08	RONALD C. GRANT	....	Died in France an Officer of the Royal Engineers
1908–09	DALLAS S. FALCONER	....	Naval Surgeon
1909–10	GEORGE M. MARTIN	....	Medical Practitioner
1910–11	W. GORDON ROBSON	....	Medical Practitioner
1911–12	ARTHUR S. CLARK	....	Indian Civil Service
1912–13	DAVID MILNE	....	(Sir) Permanent Under-Secretary for Scotland
1913–14	DONALD M. BROWN	....	Killed in action
1914–15	ROBERT M. MILLAR	....	Began as medical student. Forced to give up by ill-health. Now in business
1915–16	{ DAVID C. BUCHAN	....	Solicitor
	DAVID W. MUNRO	....	Head of Technical Research Department B.S.A.
1916–17	GEORGE M. THOMSON	....	Author
1917–18	{ THOMAS S. HAMILTON	....	Schoolmaster
	ROBERT B. HUSBAND	....	Schoolmaster
1918–19	GEORGE D. MEREDITH	....	Actuary
1919–20	WILLIAM F. ARBUCKLE	....	Civil Servant, Assistant Secretary Scottish Education Department
1920–21	{ DOUGLAS L. GOWER	....	Died 1927, Graduate of Edinburgh and McGill
	JAMES J. IMLAY	....	Inspector of Taxes
1921–22	ROBERT J. P. HARVEY	....	Civil Servant (Director of Telecommunications G.P.O.)
1922–23	WILLIAM J. WALLACE	....	Managing Director of Mac Fisheries, etc.
1923–24	JAMES C. CORSON	....	Assistant Librarian Edinburgh University
1924–25	BARCLAY S. FRASER	....	Inspector of Schools
1925–26	HENRY H. CORRIGALL	....	Medical Practitioner
1926–27	{ ERIC N. BEETON	....	Family Business—Hull
	DAVID H. C. READ	....	Chaplain to University of Edinburgh
1927–28	GEORGE W. YULE	....	Civil Servant
1928–29	WILLIAM A. T. MORTON	....	Inspector of Taxes
1929–30	MAURICE R. EWING	....	Professor of Surgery, Melbourne
1930–31	JAMES B. SCOTT	....	Medical Practitioner
1931–32	JOHN D. A. MACNICOL	....	Professor of New Testament Greek (Australia)
1932–33	{ IAN H. MACDONALD	....	I.C.S. till 1947. Now a Writer to the Signet
	WILLIAM E. THOMSON	....	Principal Scientific Officer in P.O. Engineering Department (Research Station)
1933–34	MATTHEW H. W. FRASER		Killed in Action
1934–35	RONALD P. FRASER	....	Civil Servant
1935–36	ARTHUR A. MATHESON	....	Professor of Scots Law in St Andrews University
1936–37	JAMES A. WHYTE	....	Minister
1937–38	THOMAS RARITY	....	Civil Servant
1938–39	JOHN B. MARSHALL	....	Actuary
1939–40	WILLIAM J. L. BURNS	....	Schoolmaster
1940–41	JAMES BARR	....	Professor of New Testament Literature in Montreal College of Presbyterian Church
1941–42	WILLIAM J. G. McDONALD		Minister
1942–43	STUART A. GRANT	....	Killed in Action
1943–44	THOMAS B. FLEMING	....	Actuary

1944–45	STEPHEN T. H. WRIGHT	Assistant Librarian, Scottish Central Library
1945–46	GERALD A. DICKSON	Schoolmaster
1946–47	ERIC R. MANSON	Civil Engineer
1947–48	THOMAS E. DICKSON	Medical Practitioner
1948–49	STANLEY M. SIMPSON	M.A.
1949–50	DAVID D. GALLOWAY	M.A.
1950–51	JOHN W. WIGHTMAN	Magistrand of St. Andrews University
1951–52	ALAN J. ROY	Undergraduate
1952–53	DAVID B. FAIRLIE	Undergraduate
1953–54	ROBIN A. MCLAREN	Undergraduate.

APPENDIX F.

SOME RUGBY FIGURES.

Seven-a-side victories since the war:—

1946	JEDFOREST	1951	LANGHOLM
1948	MURRAYFIELD		
	JEDFOREST	1952	GALA
	LANGHOLM		HAWICK

On three occasions we have contested the final at Melrose

Post-war Inter-city Representatives:—

1947 R. KOREN

1948 R. KOREN, W. McLENNAN, C. ROSS, S. T. H. WRIGHT

1950 E. ANDERSON, J. M. R. GIBB

1951 E. ANDERSON, S. T. H. WRIGHT

1952 T. G. WEATHERSTONE, S. T. H. WRIGHT

1953 T. G. WEATHERSTONE, K. R. MACDONALD, S. T. H. WRIGHT

1954 T. G. WEATHERSTONE, C. ROSS, W. K. L. RELPH, C. Y. LANGLANDS
(J. A. C. GILBERT, K. R. MACDONALD, J. C. M. SHARP AND S. T. H.
WRIGHT played in other District Games)

INTERNATIONALISTS

											Caps
F. KENNEDY	E	1920 1921	I	1920	W	1920	F	1920			
											5
J. C. R. BUCHANAN....	E	1921 1922 1923 1924	I	1921 1922 1923 1924 1925	W	1921 1922 1923 1924	F	1923 1924 1925			16
J. W. SCOTT	E	1925 1926 1927 1928 1929	I	1925 1926 1927	W	1925 1926 1927 1928	F	1925 1926 1927 1928 1930	NSW	1927	18

W. C. C. Agnew			I 1930	W 1930				2
M. S. Stewart	E	1933 1934	I 1932 1933 1934	W 1932 1933 1934	SA 1932			9
J. B. Borthwick			I 1938	W 1938				2
E. Anderson	E	1947	I 1947					2
S. T. H. Wright	E	1949						1
T. G. Weatherstone	E	1952 1953 1954	I 1953 1954	W 1954	F 1954 1955	NZ	1954	9
W. K L. Relph	E	1955	I 1955	W 1955	F 1955			4

68

APPENDIX G.

STEWART'S COLLEGE CLUB PAST PRESIDENTS

GEORGE C. STENHOUSE	1901–1907
A. E. GOODWIN	1907–1908
R. W. HEPBURN	1908–1910
J. ERSKINE DODS	1910–1911
JOHN GUNN	1911–1913
D. M. D. YULE	1913–1916
GEORGE W. ADAMS, ...	1916–1920
DAVID ALLAN	1920–1921
JOHN McGREGOR	1921–1922
R. K. KINNINMONT	1922–1923
H. HAMILTON BEATTIE	1923–1924
JOHN BOWIE	1924–1925
JOHN W. HAY	1925–1926
S. RUTHERFORD MACPHAIL	1926–1927
JAMES FAIRBAIRN	1927–1928
GEORGE COULL	1928–1929
WM. HOPE FOWLER	1929–1931
J. CAMERON SMAIL	1931–1933
SIR W. W. McKECHNIE	1933–1935
SIR WILLIAM Y. DARLING, ...	1935–1937
W. HAMILTON GRAY, ...	1937–1941
VERY REV. C. W. G. TAYLOR, ...	1941–1947
T. DUNBAR ADIE	1947–1948
TOM CURR	1948–1949
SIR GORDON LETHEM	1949–1951
A. V. SCOTT	1951–1952
MARK STEWART	1952–1953
A. M. McNAB	1953–1954
SIR DAVID MILNE	1954–1955